KING LEAR

Springboard Shakespeare Series

Ben Crystal

Advisory Editor, Professor Michael Dobson, Shakespeare Institute,
University of Birmingham

Macbeth
King Lear
Hamlet
A Midsummer Night's Dream

Further titles in preparation

ARDEN SHAKESPEARE
SPRINGBOARD SHAKESPEARE

KING LEAR

BEFORE | DURING | AFTER

BEN CRYSTAL

BLOOMSBURY

LONDON • NEW DELHI • NEW YORK • SYDNEY

Bloomsbury Arden Shakespeare
An imprint of Bloomsbury Publishing Plc

50 Bedford Square	1385 Broadway
London	New York
WC1B 3DP	NY 10018
UK	USA

www.bloomsbury.com

First published 2013

British Library Cataloguing-in-Publication Data
A catalogue record for this book is available from the British Library.

ISBN: PB: 978-1-4081-6467-9

Library of Congress Cataloging-in-Publication Data
A catalog record for this book is available from the Library of Congress

Typeset by Fakenham Prepress Solutions, Fakenham, Norfolk NR21 8NN
Printed and bound in Great Britain

CONTENTS

HOW BEST TO USE THIS BOOK

If you've just picked it up and you're heading into the theatre:
Take a quick look at the Relationship Circle on the inside front cover. It will give you a quick reference guide to how the characters in the play you're about to see or read relate to each other; the list of characters is on the inside back cover

- at the Interval, take a look at the Five Interval Whispers (pp.28–30)
- and just in case, the last pages of the book are a dictionary of all the difficult words in the play
- then on your way home, read through the AFTER section, which is written as a more advanced, in-depth discussion of some of the characters and issues in the play. I make reference to other characters in other Shakespeare plays, but no prior knowledge of these others is necessary

If you're about to read the play, then
- read the BEFORE section. It gives all the essential information you need about the way Shakespeare writes, and explains some of the trickier aspects of the play. It also explains the conventions of the DURING section
- the DURING section looks at theatrically interesting parts of each scene to look out for. Important character choices or difficult words and phrases are provided, and the major speeches in the play are broken down and annotated as an actor might do in a rehearsal script
- then dive into the AFTER section

If you're about to watch a film of the play, then the DURING section can be used like a DVD commentary

The book, as the title of the series suggests, is not meant to be comprehensive. The opinions are my own, and are just that – opinions. I hope they'll provoke some healthy disagreement

SERIES PREFACE

Shakespeare was written to be learnt. To be spoken out loud. So what are the things it would be useful to know before reading or watching a Shakespeare play? What few pieces of information can help turn it from being a famous work of literature into an exciting, thrilling piece of drama, that will make the experience a little bit easier, and perhaps a little more involving? What does *this* Shakespeare play mean here, tonight, now?

And when it's over, what next? These plays have been performed for over four hundred years, and they're still being performed because they're open to such wide interpretation when it comes to staging them. Director and actors need to find their own answers to the questions which Shakespeare's scripts leave wide open:

- is Hamlet actually mad or only pretending to be?
- is the Fool in *King Lear* an old man or a young boy?
- how old are the Witches in *Macbeth*? What kind of costume should they wear?
- at what point does Orlando realise the truth about Rosalind in *As You Like It*?
- does Isabella agree to marry the Duke in *Measure for Measure*?

The last is one of my favourites: Isabella, wanting to join a nunnery, is nearly forced to have sex with the manipulative Angelo, but is saved by the rightful Duke. Everything is resolved, and the Duke ends the play announcing he will propose to Isabella – but Shakespeare doesn't give her a vocal response. So how should she react? Should she agree to marry the Duke, refuse, or give no answer and leave the play with the open question?

There are no definitively right or wrong answers to these types of questions, but one of the addictive things about a Shakespeare play is knowing that those questions are there at all, and coming up with your own answers. Or going to see a production and seeing how a company of players tries to answer them for you. Then going to see another production of the same play, to see how differently *that* company answers those questions.

Measure could be performed many ways. If Isabella agrees, perhaps the actors choose to show that a love has been blossoming between her and the Duke throughout the play, and she rejects the life of a nun. If she refuses, perhaps it's because the life of a nun is the only one for her. Or does the play end with a real dilemma for Isabella? A life of a nun, or life as a Duchess with the man who saved her…

And this is just *one* moment at the very end of what many consider to be a fairly tricky play. It's this tantalisingly elusive quality that keeps people producing Shakespeare's plays and everyone who plays Hamlet, or Macbeth, or Isabella will answer these questions differently.

In this series, then, you will be guided through Shakespeare's works towards particular passages and key moments to watch out for, and – much as in a rehearsal room – nudged to consider why they might be there.

This series is not a one-stop shop, a Shakespearean supermarket where you can read up on everything you need to know about a particular play. You will not find a theme-by-theme dissection here, nor a comprehensive, definitive analysis.

Rather, using different exploratory techniques throughout, we will look at the bare bones of the play, some of the questions Shakespeare has left us, and the theatrical world in which Shakespeare was writing, offering answers to hang on the skeleton. We'll see how these questions have been answered in the past, and where in the world of Shakespeare we can go next.

This is a springboard into Shakespeare.

Ben Crystal
London, 2013

With thanks to:

Michael Dobson, Eric Rasmussen, James Shapiro, James Mardock, and Rob Gander, for their notes

Dan Winder and www.IrisTheatre.com; Roberta Brown; and the actors Emma Pallant, Laura Wickham, David Baynes, Jamie Harding, Warren Rusher, Diana Kashlan, Anwar Kashlan, Matthew Mellalieu, Benjamin O'Mahoney, Damien Molony, Hilton McRae, William Sutton, and all at www.PassionInPractice.com, for the spectacular insights I pilfered

Anthony Del Col at *Kill Shakespeare!* and Kerstin Twachtmann, for their design suggestions

Kate Bellamy for the beautiful maps

My editor Margaret Bartley; Terry Woodley, Suzi Williamson, Hilary Schan, Claire Cooper, Emily Hockley and all at Arden and Bloomsbury; Kim and all at Fakenham Prepress

Cathryn Summerhayes and Becky Thomas at William Morris Endeavor

Mum and Dad, Jim, Kate, for their notes and endless support

BEFORE

Discovery consists not in seeking new landscapes, but in having new eyes.

Marcel Proust

Who's the more foolish? The fool, or the fool that follows him?

***Star Wars* (1977)**

King Lear is an epic play. It deals with the struggles of family through the lens of monarchy; it asks questions about madness, betrayal, euthanasia, and how power can lead to a blindness to truth.

It has one of the most horrific on-stage tortures in Shakespeare's canon of plays from the smallest to the biggest parts. Its characters, intensely human from the smallest to the biggest parts, go on extraordinary journeys over the course of the five Acts.

It lives in a slightly unreal England, and while it isn't based on historical events, the King takes his name from a semi-legendary King, Leir of Britain so the whole thing feels like it's in a parallel universe. Set in a medieval sort of time, adjacent to our own history, filled with castles, Queens, spies and swordfights. Modern productions can and do update the setting, moving away from the Knights of the Round Table setting to give the play a more contemporary feel; frequently against a World War, or the reshuffle of a corporation.

But it's always a land without religion or magic – where people call on their Gods and rail against their Fates – and no-one answers, where the stars predicted the future, and where a female god spins a wheel, if you're at the top of Fortune's game, you'll spin down to the bottom, where misery waits.

MONARCH

Soon after the Scottish King James VI acceded the English throne as King James I, he survived an assassination attempt by Guy Fawkes and his co-conspirators. The attempt on the King's life rocked Shakespeare's audience's world. This was an audience still recovering from the recent loss of their Queen Elizabeth I, a woman who had reigned over them for 45 years – an impressive lifespan for that time, let alone a monarch's reign.

Indeed, until he was 39, Shakespeare knew only life under Elizabeth, and in her death he not only lost a Queen; she was the patron to his theatre company, the Lord Chamberlain's Men.

In James' accession, Shakespeare's company gained royal patronage again – they were now called the King's Men – and the next two plays he wrote were *Macbeth* and *King Lear* – one primarily about the murder of a Scottish King, and this other about a King losing his grip on his throne, losing his mind, and sending the country to war with France.

For Shakespeare's audience, the King or Queen was generally considered to be God's voice on Earth, and the removal of the rightful monarch meant anarchy, that the skies would darken and fall. This in a time when the power of superstition meant that the average audience member genuinely believed in Pixies, Faeries, and Ghosts; while the presiding religion taught that earthquakes were the punishing Hand of God.

With *King Lear*, we see a King with God-like power in a land that seems subject to the principle of Fortune – a world of loss and gain where it is no longer rightful succession but Fate that places monarchs on thrones. The lead part is considered to be the final jewel in a Shakespearean actor's crown. It's not the largest male part in Shakespeare's play – only the eighth largest – but the character's slow-motion plunge into madness and heartbreaking return to sanity are a monumental challenge for a young actor, and a fairly large mountain for an older one.

When you have the strength for it, you're too young, when you've the age, you're too old. It's a bugger isn't it?

Sir Laurence Olivier (1907–89)

A FEW BACKGROUND NOTES TO THE PLAY

• As he did for many of his plays, Shakespeare took the basic plot from Raphael Holinshed's *Chronicles* – a history of Britain whose second edition appeared in 1587, around the time Shakespeare came to London to begin his theatrical career. Shakespeare's play was the first to give the story a tragic ending – before his version, the story ended happily

• One of Shakespeare's contemporaries, Edmund Spenser, wrote a poem in 1590 called *The Faerie Queene*. It also includes the story of Lear and his daughters

• Written towards the end of Shakespeare's play-writing career, the only reference to a performance of the play is in Whitehall, London, before the court of King James I on 26th December 1606

The play was first published in 1608 as *The True Chronicle of the History of the Life and Death of King Lear and His Three Daughters*. A different version (see AFTER, pp.97–8) was published as *The Tragedy of King Lear*, around 17 years after it was first performed, in a collection compiled by two actors who had worked with Shakespeare throughout his time in London.

Originally called *Mr William Shakespeares Comedies, Histories & Tragedies*, but often referred to as the First Folio, the collection was published in 1623, seven years after his death. It gave people the chance to own 18 of Shakespeare's plays that had never been printed before, including *Macbeth, The Tempest, Antony and Cleopatra* and *Twelfth Night*.

Lear had appeared in a cheaper published form, the First Quarto of 1608, which is quite different from the version printed in the First Folio (see AFTER, p.95), a few years after it was first perfomed.

The plays were written for a skilled team of craftsmen (women weren't allowed to act until half a century later) that the writer worked with for over 15 years, and who have been referred to as 'Shakespeare's understanders like never before or since'.

They were meant to be performed live, and the characters speak directly to us, sharing the present moment, but at the same time half-belonging in a story that's been told many times over the centuries.

So while *reading* a Shakespeare play can be a struggle, understanding the shorthand Shakespeare used to help his actors can help a modern audience more easily break open the plays. The best form of introduction is to see one acted.

THE THEATRE

If you're going to see a staged production of *King Lear*, it's likely that the environment that you see it in will be very different from the way Shakespeare's audience first saw it. Once, it would have been performed around 2 p.m. in an outdoor theatre with people standing around the stage; outdoors in the yard of a tavern; or in a hall at Court, at one of the monarch's palaces. The legal fiction was that any performance at a public theatre was technically a rehearsal and preparation before showing the play to the royal patron. Still, many of Shakespeare's plays were first performed at the Globe theatre, an open-roofed, octagonal space on the south bank of the River Thames in London.

A reconstruction of the theatre opened in 1997, a hundred metres away from the original site, which tries to recreate the experience Shakespeare's audience would have had when the plays were performed in the afternoon. The lack of a roof over the yard allows the matinees to be lit by daylight; the stage is artificially lit at night, but only to simulate bright daylight.

Modern Shakespeare productions are more often staged in outdoor amphitheatres, or black-box studio theatres, or proscenium-arch theatres (where the line between the audience and the stage is very clear), old warehouses, or just about anywhere else you could imagine, and the type of theatre will have a direct effect on the production.

Depending on how well-funded or literal-minded the theatre is, there might be lighting and sound effects to replicate the storm on the Heath; or there may only be simple makeup and musical instruments used. Some modern productions will encourage audience interaction, with pantomime-like asides (when the actors talk directly to the spectators), though this tends to happen more when the audience is surrounding the stage (in the round) or on either side (in the traverse).

At the reconstructed Globe, the actors often enter or exit through the yard, and sometimes act out scenes in it, amongst the audience. Similarly, in the RSC's Elizabethan-style indoor theatres in Stratford-upon-Avon, there are walkways built in through the audience area for the actors to use, equally giving the impression of watching the action from within the world of the play.

THE PLAY

The play opens with the Dukes of Kent and Gloucester, two members of the King's Court, discussing the intended marriage between the King's favourite daughter, Cordelia, and either the King of France or the King of Burgundy.

Lear then does something strange: he demands his daughters tell him (in front of the rest of the Court) how much they love him; in return, he will give them their share of his kingdom now, to reign over, while he keeps the title of the King.

It's a foolish idea, and when Cordelia refuses to go along with this whim, he immediately turns against her. He banishes her, then his most trusted advisor, and decides to live month-by-month with his eldest daughters, who will take control of the country. When the two daughters turn against him, he goes on an amazing journey of self-discovery, culminating in the now legendary Storm (or Heath scene) where he shouts and screams his anger and frustrations at the building storm with the words: *Blow, winds, and crack your cheeks, rage, blow / you cataracts and hurricanoes…*

Meanwhile, the Duke of Gloucester, one of the King's advisors, is betrayed by his bastard son, and goes on a similar journey of self-discovery, until the two characters meet and the plot lines intertwine in the fourth Act of the play.

The heath scenes, out in the wilds of Nature, sit at the heart of the play. The words *nature*, *natural* and *unnatural* occur 50 times and over the course of the action we see children betray and rule over their parents, moving against the natural way of things.

We see a King spectacularly fall from grace: an absolute, fearful ruler is betrayed by his children; he becomes a naked old man lost in the wilderness; virtually undone by madness; shouting in the heart of a titanic thunderstorm while Nature itself, almost in pity, echoes the turmoil in his mind.

SHAKESPEARE'S WORDS

If you're reading the play, it's worth bearing in mind this fact: the plays were not intended to be read. It's said that 80 per cent of Shakespeare's audience couldn't read, and if you're not used to reading them, they can be daunting when you open the book for the first time.

There's a common idea that Shakespeare wrote in a different language, and that the plays are full of difficult words, but only about 5 per cent of all the words in Shakespeare's works are difficult for a modern audience to understand. He was writing in an early version of our modern English, and so not that much has changed.

That said, the plays are four centuries old now, so some words have changed their meaning, and we need to know what they are. The quick-reference glossary at the back of the book will help with these.

Shakespeare was writing for an audience with a different educational and cultural background, and so some references do need to be explained. When Lear, arguing with Kent, swears by Apollo and then by Jupiter, it's a great character note that he is calling – *actually* calling – on the god of the sun, of poetry, music, archery and of healing, to help him; and then when he gets *really* angry, he calls on the supreme Roman god, Jupiter, the god of thunder and lightning.

Shakespeare was the inventor – or at least the first recorded user – of over a thousand words in the English language that we still use today. He had a great gift for linguistic creation, bringing the phrase 'to elbow' someone out of the way, 'to dislocate' a bone, or 'to be untender' into the language; his audience would have been excited to hear the phrase for the first time, and it would have kept them on their toes, and listening keenly.

In the same way, when we hear unfamiliar words in a Shakespeare play they can be challenging – and maybe exciting – to us. Words like *bemonster, unpossessing, revengive, squinny* and *felicitate* float through the play, all words Shakespeare invented, that didn't make it to us, but are relatively easy to get the sense of when spoken in context.

The use of the names of people and places can be surprising too; the noblemen are referred to using the names of the parts of the country they govern over – such as Kent, Albany and Cornwall. It's hard to divine a person-ality from a name like this, but think of these titles as character notes: Kent is the solid seat of England, Cornwall is a long, thin and spiky part of England, Albany is an old name for England, bringing the idea of reliability. See the Map below (p.22) for more.

BASE, BASTARD, BASE...
Gloucester has two sons: a 'legitimate' son (i.e. a son he had with his wife), Edgar, and an 'illegitimate' or bastard son (i.e. a son he had with a woman he wasn't married to, possibly a woman he was seeing while he was married), Edmund.

Edmund has a speech where he talks about the unfairness of the fact that society dictates that he shall inherit no lands, title, or monies. Essentially the world thinks that he, an illegitimate child, is lower in nobility – base – in comparison to Edgar.

So in order to be considered worthy of inheritance, arguably, you have to somehow make yourself seem more worthy and noble than the legitimate child...

SHAKESPEARE'S THEATRE
The Globe was a roundish building – in his *Henry V*, Shakespeare describes his theatre as 'a wooden O' – and the audience sat or stood around three sides of the stage. The cheapest entrance fee would let you stand near the stage. These audience members (referred to by Hamlet as 'the groundlings') would be

packed in there, along with prostitutes, beer-sellers and pick-pockets. The most expensive seats were in the upper gallery, farthest from the stage, nearer to the fresh air and away from the hustle and bustle.

Despite the dramatic conclusion of the film *Shakespeare in Love* where Queen Elizabeth is seen to watch a play at the Globe, the monarch would never have deigned to visit such a place. As they were referred to at the time, the theatres were the home of 'rogues and vagabonds' and often doubled as venues for the 'sport' of bear-baiting (tying a bear up and letting dogs attack it until it died).

As the plays would be performed at about 2 p.m. any scenes set at night – and some of the scenes in *Lear* are – meant the actors have to act as though it was dark, and carry flaming torches. Shakespeare didn't ever prescribe an interval; it was the normal course in Elizabethan open-air theatres like the Globe to run the play through without one – refreshments (beer and nuts) were sold throughout. Later in his career, Shakespeare's company would also play at the indoor Blackfriars Theatre, where there would normally be a brief interval after every act to lower the chandeliers and refresh the candles, but no fixed break was ever set.

Lear is one of the longest plays in the canon, and even in heavily cut productions, an interval is normally inserted. In recent productions it's been placed towards the end of Act 3, at the end of the Heath scenes, chiming with the Fool's departure from the play, Lear's rescue by Gloucester and Kent, and Edgar relinquishing his disguise as Poor Tom.

NATURE & FORTUNE

There aren't any ghosts in *King Lear*. Nothing supernatural happens. There is no call for an upper stage – the balcony or roof-trap door that features in Shakespeare's Globe – nor indeed a lower one – the trap-door leading beneath the stage. It is literally a levelling play, that makes everyone equal, where King and nobleman are brought down to the plane of the commoner.

There is a surprisingly disenchanting absence of religion in the play, too. There *are* references to a 'heaven' of sorts, but they come in two distinct and unusual (in that they're not especially British) ways:

– Gloucester's astrological worrying (and Edmund's mockery of it)
– and Lear and Kent's calling on the Roman planetary gods

Unlike the end of *Cymbeline* or *As You Like It*, the characters in this play can't rely on the gods to come down and help them. In *Macbeth* and *Hamlet*, a ghost appears when the true and rightful successor hasn't taken over. This doesn't happen in *King Lear*; instead we see the King fall into the hands of Nature, facing humanity with all its naked truth and grimy reality.

Fortune is referred to over a dozen times in the play. Depicted as a blind-folded woman on a moving wheel, the idea was that as some people rise to experience great fortune, on the opposing side of Fortune's wheel others will sink to great misery (see AFTER, p.93).

THE CLIFF SCENE

King Lear was one of the first professional productions of Shakespeare I saw when I was still in school, and the scene often referred to as the Cliff scene flummoxed me. If you haven't seen the play before, the scene, played out on a flat stage, can be a little confusing.

Edgar, disguised as Poor Tom the beggarman, leads his blinded father Gloucester to the edge of a cliff in Dover. Gloucester, unaware he has been reunited with his son, intends to commit suicide by throwing himself over the edge.

Edgar leads Gloucester over flat ground, pretending to have walked up an incline to the cliff edge; he hopes the 'miraculous survival' will convince his father that he is meant to live. He describes the view, pretends to leave and Gloucester hurls himself over what he believes is the 'precipice'. Edgar then 'returns', now vocally disguising himself as a local seaman, and tells Gloucester that the beggarman who led him to the 'cliff' looked like a devil.

SHAKESPEARE'S LINES

I'm going to introduce you to Shakespeare's writing style through acting eyes. It's more often examined with a literary bent, but as his writing was originally created for actors to perform, the lines can be more easily accessible using techniques familiar to the theatrical world.

You don't *have* to understand the way verse works in order to enjoy the plays, but if you do, it will change the way you read Shakespeare for ever. He found a way to use the poetry he wrote to direct his actors, giving them notes on mood and emotion, a road-map through a speech.

Shakespeare's writing comes in several forms, and an understanding of the two main varieties is crucial: he writes in *prose*, which is a theatrical reflection of everyday speech, and he writes in poetry, organising a character's speech into rhythmical lines of *verse* – a theatrical version of intelligent, considered of highly emotional speech.

Many of the characters in *King Lear* speak in verse, but 27 per cent of the lines in the play are prose. We hear Lear, Edgar, Edmund, Gloucester, the Fool, speak in prose; Regan and Goneril tend not to, there are only a few instances where they speak in prose, usually to each other.

Prose is the speech form normally associated with Shakespeare's lower-class characters. Upper-class characters normally speak in verse; they can and do speak in prose, but when they do, they're often consciously choosing to use this more colloquial level of speech.

The King and the nobility often speak in the form of verse that was most popular in Shakespeare's lifetime: *iambic pentameter*. This was understood to be a line of rhythmical poetry (*metre*) with 10 syllables, made up of five (*penta*) stronger *DUM* beats and five weaker *de* ones, with the stronger beat every second syllable – de-**DUM** – known as an *iambic* rhythm.

Rather than write de-**DUM**, another way of annotating these beats is with an *x* for the weaker beat, and a \ for the stronger. So a line of iambic pentameter can look like this:

de **DUM** de **DUM** de **DUM** de **DUM** de **DUM**

Or this:

x \ x \ x \ x \ x \

They say the saxophone is the instrument closest in sound to the human voice; iambic pentameter is the writing closest in rhythm to spoken English, and its weak-strong beat pushes the speaker towards the more important syllables in a line. In its most regular form, we hear it when Lear speaks to his daughter Goneril:

de **DUM** de **DUM** de **DUM** de **DUM** de **DUM**
I **pri**thee, **daugh**ter, **do** not **make** me **mad**

That rhythm pushes you towards the more important words in the line, and mirrors the natural rhythm of English:

I **went** to **town** to **buy** a **coat** to**day**
de **DUM** de **DUM** de **DUM** de **DUM** de **DUM**
x \ x \ x \ x \ x \

This length of line of can be easily said with one intake of breath, and the regular heartbeat-like rhythm makes it easy to commit to memory. As we'll see, it's also a poetic style that is easy to manipulate. And Shakespeare used it to delve into the heart and the mind, and explore what it is to be human.

CHARACTERFUL SPEECH

I mentioned above that Shakespeare wrote his characters' speech in several different forms. These forms are used to convey underlying notes to the character or the subject they're talking about. Low-status characters speak in prose, a form of writing reflecting normal speech. More important characters, or more important subject matter, are given a form of speech with more style – it's stylistically heightened speech, essentially, more poetic. Look at it this way:

Regular speech – **prose** – often used amongst low-status characters

EDGAR

Who gives anything to Poor Tom? whom the foul fiend hath
led through fire and through flame, through ford and whirlpool,
o'er bog and quagmire...

Heightened speech – **iambic pentameter**, aka **verse**, aka **blank** (because it doesn't rhyme) **verse** – often used amongst high-status characters, and most easily identifiable by a capital letter at the beginning of each line

LEAR

Meantime we shall express our darker purpose.
Give me the map there. Know that we have divided
In three our kingdom;

Very heightened speech – **rhyming verse** – often used amongst high-status characters in important or emotional moments

EDGAR

The weight of this sad time we must *obey*;
Speak what we feel, not what we ought to *say*.

We don't encounter it in *King Lear*, but in other plays he gave characters speech that is even more heightened than rhyming verse – using the structure of an English poem called a **sonnet**. Higher than the sonnet, in terms of the importance or emotion underlying what's being said, is **song**, often used by the Fool.

Rhyming couplets can be indicators of particular *types* of important moments. Listen out for these couplets – they're not just poetry and nice on the ear. Sometimes they're used to indicate a character is exiting, or wanting to exit:

EDMUND

Let me, if not by birth, have lands by *wit*;
All with me's meet that I can fashion *fit*.

Also, English pronunciation has changed over the last 400 years, so bear the following example from the Fool in mind if the rhyme seems to falter (as it now does in some modern English accents):

FOOL

She that's a maid now, and laughs at my *departure*,
Shall not be a maid long, unless things be cut *shorter*.

Departure (pronounced like 'deh-part-ur') would have rhymed with *shorter* at the time Shakespeare was writing, but tends not to with the accents most commonly associated with Shakespeare performance over the last 100 years.

SIDE-NOTE – *O*

Arguably, the most important word Shakespeare uses. The single letter O is the playwright asking the actor to express an emotion of some kind. But one that fits with the context of what is being said. Surprise, anger, frustration, love… the options are limitless.

THOUGHTS VS SENTENCES

When looking at Shakespeare's writing, it makes sense to think of the play as being full of speeches to be spoken out loud, rather than text to be read: we speak in thoughts; we write in sentences.

There are never absolute rules in Shakespeare, particularly for a time when punctuation and printing were far from being standardised, and there's often disagreement between different editors of Shakespeare's texts as to where the end of a thought may lie. For the purposes of this book, thoughts end in a full stop, a question mark, or an exclamation mark. In the extracts used throughout, I'll mark where I think a thought ends by underlining the <u>last few words.</u>

A thought can finish at the end of a line of metre, like this:

LEAR
Come not between the dragon <u>and his wrath.</u>

When the end of a thought coincides with the end of a line of metre, it implies a calm, collected state of mind, contained by the poetic style. But a thought can also flow over many lines of metre – and end halfway through a metrical line. Take one of Lear's opening speeches:

LEAR
Come not between the dragon <u>and his wrath.</u>
I loved her most, and thought to set my rest
On her <u>kind nursery.</u> Hence and <u>avoid my sight!</u>
So be my grave my peace as here I give
Her father's <u>heart from her. Call France! Who stirs?</u>
<u>Call Burgundy!</u> Cornwall and Albany
With my two daughters' dowers <u>digest the third.</u>

The notion here is that the thought is too big to be contained by the metre, perhaps indicating confusion or excitement, and so the character overwhelms the style, refusing to be contained by it. Shakespearean actors are encouraged to carefully give a rising intonation to their voice in these cases, to make it clear that while the metrical line has finished, the thought hasn't:

Cornwall and Albany
With my two daughters' dowers <u>digest the third.</u>

Delivering the metre in this way can make us question *where* Lear was intending to 'set his rest', and gives extra weight to 'her kind nursery':

> I loved her most, and thought to set my rest
> On her <u>kind nursery.</u>

If a part of a thought needs to be quoted, a / is used to show where the metrical line ends. So the line above would look like this: *I loved her most, and thought to set my rest / On her kind nursery.*

BREAKING DOWN A SPEECH

In the DURING section of the book, I've used some of the analytical tools actors use to help break open a character's speech, and begun to explore what might be happening in them.

Whatever the edition of the text you might be reading, a glance at the end of each thought can make for a quick reference guide to what the speech is about:

> Come not between the dragon <u>and his wrath.</u>
> I loved her most, and thought to set my rest
> On her <u>kind nursery.</u> Hence and <u>avoid my sight!</u>
> So be my grave my peace as here I give
> Her father's <u>heart from her. Call France! Who stirs?</u>
> <u>Call Burgundy!</u> Cornwall and Albany
> With my two daughters' dowers <u>digest the third.</u>

A quick count of

– how many lines a speech is made up of
– how many separate thoughts are within those lines
– how many of those thoughts end mid-line
– and how many of the thoughts are questions

can equally give an idea as to what type of speech it is, and perhaps an insight into the character's state of mind. Characters who exclaim or ask questions are in a different state of mind from those who don't exclaim, and need no answers. Speeches with many thoughts indicate a mind moving quickly – perhaps less thoughtfully.

A speech full of longer thoughts indicates a mind more settled. A speech with many mid-line endings indicates a frantic, less composed state of mind – switching from subject to subject, the characters are interrupting themselves.

So, looking again at Lear's speech above:

– it's a 7-line speech
– which contains 8 thoughts

- 4 end mid-line
- 3 are exclaimed, and another is a question

From the exclamations and the fact that there are more thoughts than there are lines, many of which end mid-line, I know – without even looking at what Lear is *saying* – that his mind is racing, that he's excited or upset about something, and keeps switching subjects, a King lacking grace and composure at this moment.

Next to some of the speeches in the DURING section there might be a **+1** or **+2** next to the line. I'll explain what these mean in the AFTER section of the book.

MIND THE GAP

In the examples of verse above, there are ten syllables in each line. That should be true for every line of poetry written in this *iambic pentameter* form, and much of *Lear* is written in this way. When it changes (for example, when there are eight syllables, or two, or one in a line) *something* is going on in Shakespeare's writing.

In 1:1, Lear banishes his daughter Cordelia, and Kent tries to intervene:

	LEAR
1–7	As thou my sometime daughter.

	KENT
8–10	Good, my liege –

	LEAR
2 (8–10)	Peace, Kent! (x \ x \ x \ x \)
10	Come not between the dragon and his wrath.

A gap in the metre (indicated by the grey tint and marking the missing beats) gives space for a movement or reaction of some kind.

Kent has a shared line with Lear, immediately trying to change Lear's mind. Lear interrupts and quietens him, with *Peace Kent!*, and a gap of 8 beats is left to fill. It gives the actors on stage a moment to show the audience what they're thinking – a reaction shot – as they show surprise, or shock, or any number of emotions at their King's anger.

Later, in 3:7, Cornwall and Regan interrogate Gloucester, and a moment of hesitation has been written in on the 8th beat before Gloucester's answer:

	GLOUCESTER
10	I have a letter guessingly set down
10	Which came from one that's of a neutral heart
6	And not from one opposed.

CORNWALL	
7-8	Cunning.
REGAN	
9-10	And false.
CORNWALL	
1-7	Where hast thou sent the King?
GLOUCESTER	
(8), 9–10	(x) To Dover.

Gloucester's first lines have ten syllables in them, as they should. His third line only has six syllables, which means that in order to keep the iambic rhythm nice and steady, the actors playing Cornwall and Regan should speak immediately, on cue, to complete the line of metre. The staggered, stairway effect of the shared lines between Cornwall and Regan bring rapidity to the dialogue.

There are some fascinating gaps and changes in the metre in this play, and sometimes – and this just goes to show how good a dramatist Shakespeare was – it can be a space where the audience might laugh or gasp, or where characters can exit:

LEAR	
10	Thou hast her France; let her be thine, for we
10	Have no such daughter, nor shall ever see
10	That face of hers again. Therefore begone,
10	Without our grace, our love, our benison.
6 (7–10)	Come, noble Burgundy. (x \ x \ )

Flourish. Exeunt Lear, Burgundy, Cornwall, Albany, Gloucester and attendants.

FRANCE
7 (8–10)	Bid farewell to your sisters. (\ x \ )

This last gap after France's instruction is there perhaps to give Cordelia a moment, as she decides exactly what she might say to her duplicitous sisters.

SHARED LINES
When you're reading the play, you'll notice that a line sometimes begins halfway across the page, like this:

LEAR
        Hear me, recreant
On thine allegiance, hear me.

The spacing indicates half a line of metre, known as a *shared line*. This is when one line of metre – or thought – is split or shared by two or more characters. Over the course of his career, Shakespeare made more and more of his characters speak in this way. They were not obviously laid out in print as shared lines until the 1780s, but this is the norm in modern editions.

By the time he wrote *King Lear*, around a fifth of the lines in his plays were shared (compared to almost none in his earlier works). He realised that splitting the lines in this way makes for rapid-fire, pacy interaction – essentially one character interrupting or sharing the space of a thought with another.

In Act 1 Scene 1 (from here on I'll refer to particular scenes using numbers only, e.g. 1:1) Kent is objecting to Lear's actions:

KENT

| 10 | Or whilst I can vent clamour from my throat |
| 1–6 | I'll tell thee thou dost evil. |

LEAR

7–10	Hear me, recreant
6	On thine allegiance, hear me. (x \ x \)
10	That thou has sought to make us break our vow,

The numbers to the left are the number of syllables, or beats, in each line of speech. Adding the two lines together makes ten syllables, and so a full line of metre.

Splitting the line of metre between two characters means that in order to keep the rhythm bouncing along, Lear has to come in on cue, with no pause after Kent has made his bold statement. Then there's a short line of metre (*On thine allegiance, hear me*), allowing a pause for Kent to kneel, and Lear to decide his fate. It's a great writing effect, meant to bring pace and a sense of urgency to the dialogue.

In *King Lear*, Shakespeare fairly balances the shared metrical lines and switches into fast prose, with the Fool's songs, Edgar's Poor Tom ramblings and Lear's big opera-aria-like speeches scattered throughout.

THE FOOL

The Fool can be a disarming character to encounter. In medieval times it was common for a monarch to have a paid entertainer, a jester, in their Court. Some were only entertainers, but in Shakespeare's plays they have almost free rein to do and say whatever they like. Feste, the Fool in *Twelfth Night*, seems to have especial license to speak his mind, and perform for whoever he pleases.

In *Lear*, the Fool frequently speaks in riddles or song, and uses a lot of metaphor. He often comes close to stepping over the line with the things he says, but his intentions always seem to be pure: to remind Lear of the mistakes he's made, and to carefully, subtly provoke his master to think about the consequences of his actions.

With his songs and riddling speeches, the main thing to remember is that they're not nonsense and never meaningless, even if they seem to be so – the Fool, like any other character, always has a reason to speak, is always trying to affect the person he's talking to.

SIDE-NOTE

Over the course of his career, Shakespeare worked with two clowns in his troupe of actors. The first, Will Kemp, was a brilliant physical comic; the second, Robert Armin, was much more the melancholic clown and singer.

When Kemp left in 1599 Shakespeare's comedic characters went through a shift, the clown personality shifting in harmony with the change in company members. It's said the replacement clown, Armin would have improvised around the lines written for the Fool, and some modern productions allow their actor to do the same.

THOU AND YOU

This is an obscure point to modern eyes and ears, but it would have been so obvious to Shakespeare's audience it would almost be neon-lit.

In Shakespeare's time, English had two different ways of saying 'you', much like modern French. There was an informal *thou* (and its derivatives *thee, thy, thine* and *thyself*) and a formal *you* (and its derivatives *your, yours* and *yourself/ yourselves*). The distinction between these two forms was already breaking down in Shakespeare's London by the 1600s, but it seems he continued to use them as a fine dramatic device.

So whenever a character changes from one to another, it means something – perhaps a switch in attitude, a sudden flash of emotion – and considering why such a change happens, rather than dismissing it as a random or meaningless usage on Shakespeare's part, can help break open a scene.

High-status characters – Gloucester and Kent – would use *you* to each other, indicating a formal style of speech. *Thou* would be a marker of closeness – but a closeness that can mean anything from great intimacy to piercing insult.

In the relationship between Lear and Cordelia, there's a sudden shift in the way he addresses her in 1:1.

- When he asks her to change what she has said, he uses the formal *you* ('*Mend your speech a little / Lest you may mar your fortunes*'
- Then, once she has explained her reasons for not saying how much she loves him, Lear switches to the more personal *thou* ('*But goes thy heart with this?*')
- And when Cordelia persists, Lear continues to use *thou*, but it has the feeling of the less friendly version of *thou* (*Let it be so! Thy truth then be thy dower!*')

When they are finally reunited, he uses *you* to her to begin with, out of sorrow or respect, then returns to the loving, paternal *thou* when he talks to her, right up to the heart-breaking end of the play.

THE ROYAL 'WE'
One of Lear's first speeches begins like this:

LEAR
Meantime, *we* shall express our darker purpose.

He isn't announcing a group activity – it's normal practice for members of a royal family to use the majestic plural 'we' and 'our' when referring to themselves. More interesting to listen out for is when Lear's daughters, Regan and Goneril, invested with their new ruling rights, begin to use this majestic plural, slowly becoming more regal.

HUMOURS
A person's physical, mental and emotional disposition was once thought to be governed by a combination of fluids, or *humours*, within the body. Four humours were recognised: *blood, phlegm, choler* and *melancholy*.

Blood would bring passion or courage; *phlegm* would bring apathy or idleness; *choler* would bring anger or bad temper; *melancholy* would bring sadness or depression. Good health was thought to come from having the four humours in balance; if a character is behaving oddly, one of the humours is out of balance.

Lear's actions are described by Goneril as being a normal part of the *unruly waywardness that infirm and choleric years bring with them* – so his unexpected actions are blamed on an imbalance of choler in his system.

COMEDY, TRAGEDY, HISTORY...
King Lear is one of the most tragic of Shakespeare's plays, but there is great humour to be found in it too. It's often played as a tragedy with little or no comedy, and even the main 'comic' figure, the Fool, has been played as a foreboding and melancholic drunk. But as with all of Shakespeare's plays, there's an inherent balance of comedy and tragedy written in.

He knew, as the classic image of the theatre (the *persona* mask) implies, that comedy and tragedy work best next to each other. A balanced play is key: if you make the audience laugh, it'll be easier to make them cry, and vice versa. So don't be surprised if there are unexpected laughs, or if it has a black-comedy focus, instead of pure tragedy.

THE FOURTH ACT

Having started out as an actor, Shakespeare not only shaped the metre to help his troupe perform his plays, but structured the entire play with an understanding of how actors work too. So he writes in a break for his tragic lead characters.

Around Act 4 in a Shakespearean tragedy, there'll be a run of scenes that don't feature the lead: whether it be Hamlet, King Lear or Macbeth, the lead character will disappear for a while, before returning for the final climactic scenes.

In *King Lear*, Lear disappears at the end of the storm scene, and doesn't reappear until six scenes later, apparently quite mad and 'fantastically dressed'. Most of the interim scenes are quite short, and deal with the betrayal and torture of Gloucester, Goneril and Regan's tussle over Edmund, and the reintroduction of Cordelia to the plot.

THE ENDING

At the end of many recent productions of a Shakespeare play, a dance, or jig, has been performed, where everyone – dead or alive, hero and villain – comes on-stage and dances.

It signifies the end of the play, bursting the bubble of the world they'd been in for the last few hours – a particularly important function after a tragedy like *King Lear*, where the audience's emotions have been fairly wrung out. There's anecdotal evidence (from the diaries of a Swiss audience member called Thomas Platter) that Shakespeare's company did something similar to break the spell and bring everyone safely back into the real world.

The modern reconstructed Shakespeare's Globe – and others – have inserted similar dances before their final curtain call, and the catharsis that comes from this joint celebration can feel incredibly uplifting.

A WORD ON THE TEXT

Depending on which publisher's edition of the text has been used for the production, or which edition you're reading, the spellings – and indeed sometimes entire words or scenes – will appear differently; for example, Act 2:2 in the Arden text is sometimes split into three separate scenes in other editions.

In terms of staging the play, if the location doesn't need to change, if many of the same characters are involved, and there hasn't been a time-shift, then there may not be a reason to break up the scene. Edgar isn't likely to be on the run near Gloucester's castle, so perhaps the isolation of his '*I heard myself proclaimed*' speech as a separate scene – or at least a separate part of the stage from where Kent sits in the stocks – would mean no hasty scene change or moving of scenery.

Similar to *Hamlet*, there's more than one text from Shakespeare's time of *King Lear*, and they're slightly different from each other. I'll talk about these differences in AFTER (pp.97–8).

A FEW RELATIONSHIP / TITLE POINTS

Characters in Shakespeare plays often have a number of different names or titles, and it isn't always clear how they relate to each other. Similar to his History plays, many of the characters are named after the provinces that they are in charge of, and/or where their castle is:

Gloucester – the Duke* of Gloucester; the King's foreign advisor, and one of his Chief Courtiers

Kent – the Duke of Kent; a Chief Courtier and advisor to the King; sometimes played as the King's main bodyguard; later disguises himself as Caius

Albany – the Duke of Albany, husband to Lear's eldest daughter, Goneril

Cornwall – the Duke of Cornwall, husband to Lear's middle daughter, Regan

Burgundy – the King of Burgundy, suitor to Cordelia, Lear's youngest daughter

France – the King of France, suitor to Cordelia, Lear's youngest daughter

Edmund – bastard son of the Duke of Gloucester, later referred to as Gloucester

Edgar – legitimate son of the Duke of Gloucester, and godson to Lear (and so named 'Edgar' by Lear); later disguises himself as a beggar called Poor Tom O'Bedlam, and later still, a fisherman

*Duke – a member of the nobility, the highest rank below the monarch, ranking with an Earl's son, and holding lands of the king. Historical titles are hard to relate to, but a Duke can be thought as similar to a Governor in a Western cowboy film, helping reign over a section of the country for the President

LIST OF PROPS MENTIONED IN THE PLAY
(Assuming the male characters would originally already have hats, swords and/or daggers)

– *a map*
– *a coxcomb* (the cap the Fool wears, often with bells attached)
– *a pair of stocks* (a wooden structure used for punishment; it has holes to secure the offender's ankles, and sometimes the wrists; it's usually placed outside and in public)
– *a feather*

LETTERS IN LEAR

There are 17 pieces of paper, mainly letters, that pass hands between characters over the course of the play. The author of the letter can sometimes be divined from the *hand*, or *character* (writing style) of the person who wrote it:

1. Map of the Kingdom in 1:1
2. Edmund's letter in Edgar's hand in 1:2, detailing the 'plot' against Gloucester
3. Goneril's letter to Regan in 1:3, detailing the behaviour of Lear and his Knights, carried by Oswald, mentioned in 1:4, and again by Kent in 2:2
4. Lear's letters to Regan, detailing his intended arrival, taken by Kent in 1:5
5. Cordelia's letter to Kent in 2:2
6. Cordelia's letter to Gloucester in 3:3, detailing her powers landed in Dover
7. Cornwall's letter to Albany, taken by Goneril in 3:7
8. Regan's letter to Goneril in 4:2, presumably detailing Cornwall's death
9. Goneril's intended reply to Regan's letter, mentioned in 4:2
10. Kent's letters to Cordelia mentioned in 4:3, presumably part of his purse in 3:1
11. Goneril's letter to Edmund detailing their intent to kill Albany and marry each other; carried by Oswald desired by Regan in 4:5; found and read by Edgar in 4:6; given to Albany 5:1; shown to Edmund and Goneril in 5:3
12. Regan's note to Edmund in 4:5, given to Oswald
13. Lear's challenge to Cupid in 4.6
14. Edgar's cover letter to no.11, given to Albany in 5:1
15. Edmund's note to Captain in 5:3, a writ on Lear and Cordelia's lives
16. Formal duel announcement, read by the Herald in 5:3

Albany – an ancient name for North Britain; it has a solid, trustworthy ring to it

Burgundy – a eastern region of central France; famous for having very fertile lands, it wasn't known for its wine until the end of the 17th century

Cornwall – south-east corner of England; the territory of Cornwall, Regan's husband; sharp and spiky, it juts out into the cold beginnings of the Celtic sea

Dover – south England; the high white cliffs of Dover are a classic image of Britain; Cordelia's army lands here, Kent helps smuggle Lear here, and Gloucester asks the disguised Edgar to take him to a cliff-top nearby

France – only 40 kilometres across the water, England and France had been at war many times together, wars retold in many of Shakespeare's previous plays; famous for its wines, a solid union between France and England would have been well-prized; perhaps controversially for Shakespeare's audience, the French arrive in the final acts as the Good Guys

Gloucester – the neighbouring county to Shakespeare's home county of Warwickshire, and home to Bristol, the main port for trade and jumping-off point to the colonies

Kent – nicknamed the 'garden of England' since 1855; a beautiful county in the seat of south-east England, and the closest part of the country to France; its position and strength in times of war a possible character note for Kent; the county was singular in England in that it held the common law of *gavelkind*, where lands were divided equally among heirs – is Lear intentionally adopting the laws of the territory of his most loyal subject?

STAGE DIRECTIONS GLOSSARY

Each scene of the play in a modern text is preceded by a stage direction, introducing the characters, and often saying what is happening. When you go to see a theatre production, the director will have interpreted these directions for you. But if you are reading a text, you're likely to encounter the following terms:

alarum(s) – a call to arms during a battle when in war

aloud – opposite to aside; other characters can now hear the speaker

aside – in Shakespeare's time, a theatrical moment when the character speaks to the audience and the other characters usually cannot hear the speaker; in more modern times, sometimes spoken as a moment of internal reflection

colours – each army would have its own colours, shown on flags, shields and uniforms

in conquest – in a triumphant manner, having won a war or a battle

dead march – a slow, solemn walk, befitting a funeral

divers – different, various, several

draw back – move upstage, away from the audience

drum – a drum being beaten to signify an approaching army

exeunt – they exit (Latin plural of 'exit')

flourish – fanfare of horns or trumpets, usually accompanying an exit or entrance

horns within – used when hunting, and to sound the return of the hunting party

sennet – trumpet call signalling a procession

several / severally / opposite [doors] – indicates characters enter or exit at different points on the stage

sewer – chief servant, master of ceremonies

torch(es) – flaming torches to light the way, and in the Globe, to help signify night-time

with lights – holding flaming torches or candle lanterns

tucket within – a trumpet playing a particular sequence of notes; each member of royalty or the nobility would have their own tucket, allowing them to announce their imminent arrival from afar

FINAL THOUGHTS

Before you head to the theatre, turn on the film, or open the book, it's worthwhile to think about how the play you're about to experience might be staged. Would a big and varied set work best for this kind of play, or a bare stage? Should modern dress with guns be used, or costumes and weaponry from a particular period or event in history?

King Lear is loosely set in an eleventh-century version of Britain, but Shakespeare was using his country as the base foundation for the play – he wasn't creating historical fiction-theatre – so it would be false to say it *should* be set somewhere in particular.

As with all theatre, the questions to ask is

- What does this play mean here, today, tonight?
- What is in the writing that makes people still want to produce it?
- And what does each character want from each scene?

These are the kinds of questions a production's rehearsal process begins with, and your own expectations of the answers will dramatically shape your experience of *King Lear...*

People talk about the difference between radio acting, TV acting, and stage acting, but I think it's all the same. For instance when I played Vultan in Flash Gordon, I put as much energy into it as I would with King Lear – it's all part of the same thing.

Brian Blessed

DURING

FIVE INTERVAL WHISPERS

ACT 1

---

1 1:1 – Dividing the Map and Cordelia
Cordelia

Lear's youngest daughter is one of those tricky parts in Shakespeare. We see her very briefly in 1:1, and then she disappears for four acts, to return quite changed. When she stands up to her King and father at the beginning, we need to see the caring, loving, softer side to her that Lear so dearly dotes on. Equally though, we need to see the strength in her that will blossom into the Queen we meet in Act 4.

---

2 1:2 – Edmund and the family Gloucester
Edmund

Being the illegitimate child of Gloucester, Edmund will not inherit any lands when his father dies. He makes his father think that his brother Edgar is planning to murder Gloucester, and split the lands between them.

He then progresses to involve himself with Goneril (whose husband Albany is still very much alive) and with Regan (who plans to marry him after her husband Cornwall dies).

1:3 – Goneril and her steward Oswald
1:4 – Visiting Goneril and Albany
1:5 – Leaving Goneril and Albany

ACT 2
2:1 – Edgar's flight, Cornwall and Regan's arrival
2:2 – Kent and Oswald's fight
2:3 – Edgar and Poor Tom
2:4 – The ill-treatment of Lear, and his departure

ACT 3
3:1 – Storm, war and invasion with Kent
3:2 – The Storm Scene
3:3 – Gloucester confides in Edmund
3:4 – Lear and Poor Tom
3:5 – Edmund betrays Gloucester

3 3:6 – Shelter for the mad king
The disappearance of the Fool

Famously, the character of the Fool disappears halfway through the play. Sometimes played as a young boy, sometimes similar in age to Lear, his songs, riddles and many of his speeches are slightly cryptic to hear. He has his own very particular way of helping Lear to understand the world – it all makes sense when spoken by an actor who has done the work for you.

His sudden absence is often explained by the arrival of Poor Tom. Lear, drowning in madness, can no longer hear the Fool's wisdom, instead cleaving to Tom's ramblings; so realising he is of no further use, the Fool leaves.

Some productions have had him captured by soldiers and hanged, as war breaks out (first between Albany and Cornwall; then with Cordelia's French army).

3:7 – The torture of Gloucester

ACT 4
4:1 – Gloucester meets Poor Tom
4:2 – Goneril and Edmund, and Albany
4:3 – Kent and news of Cordelia's invasion
4:4 – The return of Cordelia
4:5 – Regan's attempt to seduce Oswald

4 4:6 – Gloucester's Cliff Scene, Lear's madness, and Oswald's reward
Gloucester's eyes and the 'cliff'

One of the most horrific scenes in Shakespeare's canon, the torture of Gloucester in 3:7 includes the famous line *Out vile jelly*. It offers the designer and director of a production an interesting question: how do you stage someone's eyes being ripped out?

A few scenes later, Gloucester asks a disguised Edgar to lead him to a clifftop in Dover, intending to throw himself off. Edgar tricks him out of suicide by taking him to flat ground. It's sometimes unclear this is the case – our natural instinct is to imagine there actually *is* a steep drop in front of Gloucester.

4:7 – Cordelia and Lear reconciled

ACT 5

5:1 – Edmund and Regan, Albany and Edgar

5:2 – 5:3 – War between England and France

Lear's final lines

Note the rhythm to one of Lear's final lines:

Never, never, never, never, never

It has the rhythm

DUM-de **DUM**-de **DUM**-de **DUM**-de **DUM**-de
NEV-er **NEV**-er **NEV**-er   **NEV**-er **NEV**-er

This type of verse is called *trochaic pentameter*: it has the same number of beats per line as iambic pentameter, but the rhythm of every beat is backwards (a **DUM**-de rhythm rather than the usual de-**DUM**).

At the point in the play where Lear's world is turned completely upside down, inside out and back to front, Shakespeare does the same to his verse. A brilliantly subtle character note for an actor.

Act 1:1

Location: *The Court of King Lear*

Characters: *Kent, Gloucester, Edmund, King Lear, Cornwall, Albany, Goneril, Regan, Cordelia, Attendants, King of France, King of Burgundy*

Action: *Two advisors to the King – the Dukes of Kent and Gloucester – discuss whether the King's youngest daughter, Cordelia, will choose the King of France or the King of Burgundy as her husband. Edmund, Gloucester's half-son, has just returned from some time spent travelling away, and is introduced to Kent.*

Lear arrives in Court and proceeds to divide up his kingdom. He'll give the largest part to the daughter who loves him the most, and remain King only in name. Cordelia refuses to express her love in return for land, and the King banishes her from Britain. Kent tries to interject and, after arguing with the King, is also banished.

The scene is bookended in prose – it opens with the characters talking of sex (where life begins) and children (who life becomes). Despite the subject matter, the two main speakers keep polite, calling each other Sir. They shift into the heightened language of poetry, as they should, when the King enters. The scene returns to prose, as the two elder sisters consider the age and infirmity of their father: talking, in other words, about where life ends.

The lines before Lear enters give early weight to the subplot, and subtly underscore the importance of Edmund's character – his father's storyline is of equal importance in this tragedy.

With Lear's arrival, we are – without preparation – dropped into a dramatic reversal of fortune for a number of characters. No other play in the canon does this, and Shakespeare's audience would have had to rely on its prior understanding of what constitutes good kingship, to clearly see Lear's bad decision-making.

☞ CHARACTERS BURGUNDY's milk vs FRANCE's wine

Burgundy wasn't famous for its wine until the end of the 17th century, but it wasn't famous for milk, either. It was famous for having fertile lands, with a possible character note to its King of being virile, able to father lots of princes and princesses. The wine of France, however, was prized by all, and considered to be the highest quality. England had a history of needing good alliances with France; when there wasn't a strong relationship between them they were often at war.

The red strength and perceived excellent quailty of French wine (that improves with age), against the thin, white cow or, more likely, goat's milk (that would have gone off very quickly in Shakespeare's day) give nice character notes for two very small parts.

Forming a normal part of a royal wedding, the Kings of France and Burgundy are expecting the Princess Cordelia to come with something, a gift from Lear, called a *dowry*. It would normally be a chunk of land to rule over, or a big lump of money. As he rules over a small region, Burgundy wants the piece of Britain originally promised by Lear. But France, rather romantically, says he is content with just the Princess; he says Cordelia *is herself a dowry*. But is Cordelia genuinely more keen on France? Or is it also a shrewd, political move on her part? Or a combination of both?

☞ NOTHING WILL COME OF NOTHING

Lear's response to Cordelia's 'nothing, my lord' is one of the most famous lines in the play, and one of my favourite lines in the canon. The simple idea that it is impossible to yield something from nothing is age-old, reflected in the Biblical parable of the Talents.

Lear's own expectation that he can essentially do *nothing* and still rule scrapes against his own argument, that Cordelia should say *something* to gain her share of his monarchy. The word 'nothing' is used 34 times in the play, as the thought of raising nothing from nothing gently echoes throughout the tragedy.

☞ **SIDE-NOTE**   GAP IN METRE

After Cordelia's admission, and Lear's beautifully simple reply, 'Nothing will come of nothing, speak again', Cordelia explains to her father. There's a gap in the metre before Lear can bring himself to speak, while the resolute Cordelia needs no time to reply – great character notes for both:

CORDELIA

| 11 | Sure I shall never marry like my sisters |
| 1-6 (7–10) | To love my father all. (x \ x \) |

LEAR

| 1-6 | But goes thy heart with this? |

CORDELIA

| 7-10 | Ay, my good Lord. |

···

☞ **SIDE-NOTE**   EYES, GODS, AND JUPITER

Very early in the play, we're presented with a subtly different world from our own:

LEAR

Out of my sight!

KENT

See better, Lear, and let me still remain
The true blank of thine eye. (x \ x \)

LEAR

Now by Apollo –

KENT

Now by Apollo, King
Thou swear'st thy gods in vain.

LEAR

O vassal, miscreant!

1) it places Britain in an alternate universe history, where the Christian god doesn't have a place but the Roman/Greek gods do

2) it also allows Lear a power that Shakespeare's audience believed, that the monarch was the mouthpiece through which gods spoke. Here Lear goes a step further and calls

on them directly, believing that Apollo will come down to Earth so the King can temporarily use his power.

....

☞ WORDS

- *make choice of either's* **moiety** = share; both Cornwall and Albany will be gifted equal parts of Lear's kingdom
- *our* **darker** *purpose* = secret, unrevealed (rather than the modern villainous meaning)
- *I am alone* **felicitate** = made happy; an artificial, classical word which hints at Regan's insincerity
- *our grace, our love, our* **benison** = blessing
- *the mysteries of* **Hecat** = the Greek Goddess of the Underworld, and Queen of Witches
- **propinquity** *and property of blood* = blood relationship; an incredible thing to say – Lear is denying his familial relationship with Cordelia
- *the barbarous* **Scythian** = Scythia equates geographically to modern Russia; Roman poets considered the inhabitants to be especially vicious and savage
- **check** *this hideous rashness* = recant or take back this quick and terrible decision
- *receive not alone the imperfections of* **long-ingraffed condition** = a deeply ingrained or habitual part of someone's character
- **choleric** *years* = angry (see *Humours*, p.18)
- *We must do something. And* **i'th'heat** = very soon

Act 1:2

Location: *Gloucester's Castle*

Characters: *Edmund, Gloucester, Edgar*

Action: *Some time after the first scene, and the beginnings of the subplot. Edmund, in order to be eligible for his father's inheritance, works to convince Gloucester that his brother Edgar is plotting murder.*

As far as the poetic style goes, it's the opposite of the previous scene, beginning in verse, moving into prose when Gloucester and latterly Edgar arrive, then back to verse at the end, Edmund seemingly pleased as his plot moves forward, ending in a rhyming couplet.

....

☞ CHARACTERS GLOUCESTER

Gloucester is home to Bristol, one of the most important ports in Shakespeare's time, for trade, for heading to the colonies, for international affairs. Some productions have Gloucester played not only as a royal advisor, but more as the Foreign Minister, who has put time and effort into arranging the possible union between France and Burgundy.

His line *'if it be nothing, I shall not need spectacles'* is often played to show a lovely and rare sense of humour for a character about to undergo terrible times.

⏺ SPEECH EDMUND THE BASTARD

22 lines; 16 thoughts, 9 end mid-line, 9 are questions. Two chunks in the speech where the metre indicates he is particularly emotionally charged – when he talks first of his bastardy, and when he talks of Edgar's legitimacy.

Any regular person can try to talk to the gods, but this is different from the way Lear calls on them. Edmund is calling on the goddess of the Earth – as far as he's concerned, he is natural. Social rules and custom deems him unnatural, and finding no real reason for his unfair displacement in society, he decides to improve his situation himself.

As with the most interesting dramatic characters, rather than the moustache-twirling evil villain, Edmund is right – life for him is unfair. Simply because he was born out of wedlock, society decides he is no good. As the bastard, he doesn't stand to inherit anything when Gloucester dies. He argues, in fact, that bastards are better, and have a more vigorous (fierce) quality to them than legitimately born children.

EDMUND

Thou, Nature, art my goddess; to thy law
My services are bound. Wherefore should I
Stand in the **plague of custom** and permit
The **curiosity of nations** to deprive me, +2
For that I am some twelve or fourteen **moonshines** +1
Lag of a brother? Why bastard? Wherefore base? +1
When my dimensions are as well-compact,
My mind as gen'rous, and my shape as **true**,
As honest madam's issue? Why brand they us +1
With '**base**'? with 'baseness'? 'bastardy'? 'base, base'?
Who in the lusty stealth of nature take
More composition and fierce quality
Than doth within a dull, stale, tired bed
Go to the creating a whole tribe of **fops**
Got 'tween asleep and wake? (x \ ) Well then, -2
Legitimate Edgar, I must have your land.
Our father's love is to the bastard Edmund +2
As to the legitimate. Fine word 'legitimate'. +3
Well, my ' legitimate,' if this letter speed
And my **invention** thrive, Edmund the base
Shall top the legitimate. I grow, I prosper. +1
Now gods stand up for bastards! (\ x \ ) -3

plague of custom
= the affliction of
common practice

curiosity of nations =
painstaking attention
to detail by national
law

moonshine = month

true = true to his
father's likeness

base = low-born, of
lower rank in society

fop = fool, jackass

x \ – a pause before
revealing his plan?
as he takes out the
letter?

invention = plan,
scheme

··

☞ HOROSCOPES

Gloucester talks of the 'eclipses of the sun and moon',
suggesting bad news is coming. Edmund mocks his superstition, claiming his character has nothing to do with where
the stars or planets were when he was born. But when
his brother Edgar enters, he mimics his father's worries
about the eclipses. Edgar is surprised to hear Edmund
speak in such a way – and Edmund keeps Edgar off guard
as he dupes him into thinking he has offended their father
Gloucester.

··

☞ THOU / YOU   THE GLOUCESTER FAMILY

Gloucester uses *you* throughout to Edmund, until the end of
the scene, when he tells him 'find out this villain Edmund, it

shall lose *thee* nothing', a final show of familial closeness, and perhaps the beginning of Gloucester's better treatment of his bastard son.

Edgar and Edmund stay with *you* throughout their exchange – a formality you wouldn't necessarily expect with brothers in an emotionally charged scene – but nicely indicating the distance in their relationship; that as half-brothers, they're not *that* close.

☞ WORDS

- *a* **sectary astronomical** = a devotee to astrology; one who believes there is a relationship between astronomical phenomena and human behaviour
- *all this done* / **Upon the gad** = suddenly
- *you know the* **character** *to be your brother's* = the style of handwriting
- *it is his* **hand** = his hand-writing style

Act 1:3

Location: *Goneril and Albany's household*

Characters: *Goneril, Oswald*

Action: *Lear has arrived at his eldest daughter's household for the first month-long stay. Goneril complains about the behaviour of Lear and his followers, and encourages Oswald to incite Lear to further unhappiness…*

☞ CHARACTER OSWALD

The Steward of a household – particularly a royal house – was a high-status role. In charge of the other servants, and attending to the outgoing monies, it was a position that commanded respect. Goneril's opening line is quite complicated, but is worth close attention

GONERIL
Did my father (Lear) strike my Gentleman (Oswald)
for chiding of his (Lear's) Fool?

Goneril is talking to Oswald about something that happened
to him; it's slightly odd that she refers to him in the third
person, as her Gentleman. She also refers to him as *you*, as
something of an equal. Perhaps she's flattering him, making
him feel better since he's been beaten.

Certainly, as a servant, it would be more appropriate to refer
to him as *thou*. It underlines his high status, and the status of
a Steward is something that had already caught Shakespeare's
attention, with Malvolio in *Twelfth Night*.

....

☞ CHARACTER   GONERIL

Goneril switches from prose up into verse after the opening
line. It could be argued she also switches up into the royal
'we' with the lines:

• *He flashes into one gross crime or other / That sets us all at
odds*
• *His knights grow riotous and himself upbraids us / On every
trifle*

For the rest of her speech she uses *I / my*, but this instance
of 'we' ('us/our') allows for an interesting acting choice – is
Goneril beginning to take on her royal standing?

....

☞ WORDS

• **come slack** *of former services* = be less attentive
• *old fools are babes again, and must be used / With* **checks**,
as flatteries = insults

Act 1:4

Location: *Goneril and Albany's household*

Characters: *Kent (in disguise from this scene onwards), Lear, Lear's Knights, Oswald, Goneril, Fool, Albany*

Action: *The disguised Kent arrives at Goneril's house, and in tripping up Oswald, gains service once more with the King.*

After his opening speech in verse, Kent switches down to prose when he meets the King – to show the commonness he's adopted as part of his disguise? Apart from the Fool's songs, the scene stays in the relaxed prose style until Goneril arrives and again, she switches up into poetry, bringing a formal tone back. Lear, however, nicely returns to the more common and less kingly prose when he asks Who is it can tell me who I am?, *and the Fool replies in prose* Lear's shadow.

*It's a packed scene, introducing the Fool (see below), setting up the beginnings of strain in the relationship between Albany and Goneril, giving the first sign that Lear might be aware that he did Cordelia wrong (*O most small fault*), and with his* Old fond eyes… I'll pluck you out *the foreshadowing of darker things yet to come.*

··

☞ CHARACTER KENT

The county of Kent is the part of England closest to French shores. In times of war, it required heavy defence. The man in charge of that area of land would need to be a strong, utterly loyal, and close friend to the King. Which, rather wonderfully, is exactly who Kent is.

For the disguise, as well as a change of costume, film productions have had Kent shave his head; theatre productions often use a wig or fake beard in Kent's first scene, which are removed from this scene onwards.

☞ CHARACTER THE FOOL

This is not altogether fool, my lord, says Kent, and if there was a good single character note for the Fool perhaps it would be this. A lot of what the Fool says appears to be nonsensical, but very often he is disguising parcels of wisdom – mainly aimed at making Lear see sense – as foolery, here pushing Lear to half-repeat his earlier exchange with Cordelia:

FOOL
Can you make no use of nothing, nuncle?

LEAR
Why no boy. Nothing can be made out of nothing.

The Fool and Lear's use of *thou* and *you* is interesting. They both use *thou* to each other, indicating a very close, affectionate relationship, and Goneril's description of him as being 'all-licensed' couldn't be truer – Lear gives his foolish councillor licence to do or say anything he wants.

He refers to a *coxcomb* – a fool's cap, sometimes with small bells attached, and would have been dressed in motley – a coloured, patchwork set of clothes. He often calls Lear *nuncle* – a child-like shortening of 'mine uncle'. Theirs is not a familial relationship, here *uncle* means *guardian*, or *master*.

The Fool's wisdom is often written in various styles – he frequently switches quickly up from prose to rhyming verse, and his lines are often sung. When the rhyme seems to fail, it's most likely because the pronunciation has changed over the last 400 years (see BEFORE, p.11).

○ SPEECH LEAR

15 lines; 7 thoughts, 4 of which are exclaimed, 3 ending mid-line. Metrically, a fairly regular speech, and Lear seems to gain more control towards the end.

The second character to call on the goddess Nature, although in theory Lear has the power both to make Nature hear him and to effect his curse on Goneril, making her sterile or – ironically, considering his own temperament – ensuring her offspring will be a bad-tempered child.

The idea here is of the sins of the father transferring through to the child, echoing Gloucester's relationship with his sons. Soon after this speech, Lear calls Goneril a degenerate bastard – making her as bad in Lear's mind as Edmund is considered to be?

Edmund is thought to be bad because he was born out of wedlock, but is actually good at heart. Goneril is good at heart and noble (as she is the rightful daughter of Lear and heir to the throne) but then displays the traits of which Edmund is accused…

LEAR

Hear, <u>Nature, hear!</u> Dear <u>goddess, hear!</u> (x \\)	-2
Suspend thy purpose if thou didst intend	
To make <u>this creature fruitful.</u> (\\ x \\)	-3
Into her womb convey sterility,	
Dry up in her the organs of increase,	+1
And from her **derogate** body never spring	
A babe <u>to honour her.</u> If she must **teem**,	
Create her child of **spleen**, that it may live	
And be a **thwart** disnatured <u>torment to her.</u>	
Let it stamp wrinkles in her brow of youth,	
With **cadent** tears fret channels in her cheeks,	
Turn all her mother's pains and benefits	
To laughter and contempt, that she may feel	
How sharper than a serpent's tooth it is	
To have a <u>thankless child!</u> <u>Away, away!</u>	

x \\ – as Lear waits for Nature to listen?

x \\ – as Lear prepares his curse?

derogate = degenerate
teem = give birth
spleen = bad-tempered
thwart = stubborn
cadent = falling

....

☞ WORDS

- *mar a **curious** tale in telling it* = ruin an elaborate story
- *the best of me is **diligence*** = care, caution
- *the **roundest** manner* = bluntest
- *you base **football player*** = an insult; in Shakespeare's time football was a game for lowly commoners
- *if you will measure your **lubber's** length again, **tarry*** = if you want to find out how much of a **blundering idiot** you are, **stay**

- **epicurism** *and lust* = gluttony, sensual excess
- *detested* **kite***!* = a thieving bird of prey; equivalent to modern term of abuse 'bitch'
- *well, well,* **th'event***!* = the outcome, or consequence; equivalent to 'let's see what happens'

Act 1:5

Location: *Outside Goneril's Castle*

Characters: *Lear, Kent, Fool, Knights*

Action: *Kent is sent on ahead to Regan's castle to make sure they are ready to receive the King, while the Fool gently berates Lear for his foolishness in giving up his crown to his daughters.*

☞ MADNESS

A short scene written mostly in prose, Lear switches up into verse at the first mention of madness:

> **FOOL**
> Thou shouldn't not have been old till thou hadst been wise.

> **LEAR**
> O let me not be mad, not mad, sweet heaven!
> Keep me in temper; I would not be mad.

In between the Fool's questions, as he tries to cheer Lear, and counsel him at the same time, the short line *I did her wrong* is sometimes played in relation to his recent outburst at Goneril. More often, though, it's played to carry on the previous scene's reflection towards Cordelia; a growing realisation in Lear that he made a mistake in banishing his one faithful daughter...

☞ WORDS

- *in danger of* **kibes** = blisters; an inflamed heel
- *the* **seven stars** = the pleiades; a constellation of over 1000

stars known as the *seven sisters* (as the naked eye can discern only seven), and well-known to cultures around the world, symbolising sorrow. In some versions of Greek mythology, the seven sisters killed themselves in sadness for their father Atlas, who was forced to carry the heavens on his shoulders.

Act 2:1

Location: *Outside Gloucester's Castle*

Characters: *Edmund, Curan, Edgar, Gloucester, Cornwall, Regan, Attendants*

Action: *The second part of Edmund's plot unfolds with Edgar's flight, and the first signs that his plan is working, show as he rises in social status: Cornwall makes him a part of his retinue at the end of the scene.*

At the start, Edmund meets with a servant (Curan), who tells of Cornwall and Regan's unexpected arrival at Gloucester's castle, and we hear of a conflict growing between Cornwall and Albany…

The scene is filled with the characters sharing lines of metre, bringing some much-needed pace after the previous scene's melancholic and philosophical reflections.

....

☞ CHARACTER EDMUND

In a flurry of activity and speech, Edmund dupes Edgar into fighting with him, and forces his brother to flee, saying *In cunning I must draw my sword upon you.* He doesn't give Edgar time to think. This naivety in Edgar disappears later, once he returns from the poverty of his Poor Tom disguise.

Relating Edgar's flight to his father, Edmund says *But that I told him the revenging gods / 'Gainst parricides did all the thunder bend:* using an idea that Lear profoundly believes in – that the Gods will send Nature against father-murderers – to his benefit.

☞ WORDS

- **_ear-kissing_** _arguments_ = reaching the ear only as rumours, rather than fact
- _conjuring the moon / To_ **_stand_** _auspicious mistress_ = asking the moon **to act as** his fortune-giving servant
- **_gasted_** _by the noise_ = frightened
- _I never_ **_got_** _him_ = conceived, bred; Gloucester, as Lear did in 1:1, is disclaiming his familial relationship to Edgar
- _Hark, the Duke's_ **_trumpets_**_!_ = see _tuckets_ (BEFORE, p.24)
- _I'll work the means to make thee_ **_capable_** = able to inherit; Gloucester promises to find a way to work around Edmund's bastardy; Edmund has very quickly got what he wanted in 1:2
- _I hear that you have shown your father / A child-like_ **office** = duty, service; perhaps eliciting a bitterness from Edmund, still not thought of as a true child?
- _he did_ **_bewray_** _his_ **_practice_** = he did reveal his treachery

Act 2:2

Location: _The grounds of Gloucester's Castle_

Characters: _Kent, Oswald, Edmund, Cornwall, Regan, Gloucester, Servants_

Action: _We learn (in 2:4) that Kent has come straight from Cornwall's Castle, where Oswald has been with letters from Goneril. On reading the letters, Cornwall and Regan immediately leave for Gloucester's Castle, pursued by Kent and Oswald._

The two arrive at the same time, Kent begins to beat Oswald, and after provoking Cornwall, Kent is punished by being put into the stocks for the rest of the night – a great insult to a messenger of the King, and indicative of how Cornwall sees Lear himself. Note how Kent later switches to the more formal you (Call not your stocks for me), as he mentions the King, subtly underlining Cornwall's inappropriateness.

The barrage of insults Kent throws at Oswald has become famous – it's unusual to hear someone swear so articulately these days – and it's not necessary to understand every detail of every insult; the general theme is clear even if every word isn't. Still, here are the most obscure explained.

Oswald, as the classic coward character, runs from Kent, then, once he has the protection of the Duke, begins to brag, saying his life he *spared at suit of his grey beard* – that he generously didn't kill Kent because he was old.

- **Lipsbury pinfold** = a wrestling hold
- **knave** = scoundrel, rogue
- *eater of* **broken** *meats* = leftovers; implying poverty or lowliness
- **base** = someone born of a low social ranking
- **three-suited** = someone who only has three suits to wear; a servant
- *hundred pound, filthy-***worsted**-*stocking* = socks made of a woolen fabric (and so inferior to the more expensive silk)
- **lily-livered** = weak, lacking in courage
- **action**-*taking* = someone who likes to take legal action; implying a pendantic quality
- **whoreson** = the son of a whore (prostitute); being born out of marriage, like Edmund is, meant no right to inherit from the father
- **glass-gazing** = someone who likes to admire themselves in the mirror; narcissistic
- **super-serviceable** = someone who offers service beyond what is needed; overzealous, officious
- **finical** *rogue* = fussy, nit-picking, pedantic
- *a* **bawd** *in way of good service* = a pimp or go-between; Kent accuses Oswald of being someone who greases the wheel, who helps others get what they want
- **pander** = pimp or go-between; similar to **bawd**
- *son and heir of a* **mongrel bitch** = the offspring and heir to a non-pedigree female dog
- **brazen-faced varlet** = shameless rogue
- *a* **sop** *o'the moonshine* = a piece of bread steeped in liquor, eaten before bedtime; by running Oswald through with his sword, his body will be open to soak up the moonshine

- *I'll so* **carbonado** *your* **shanks** = slash your legs
- *you whoreson* **cullionly barber-monger** = despicable frequenter of the barber-shop (= vain)
- *thou whoreson* **zed** = as in the final letter of the alphabet; considered to be relatively useless
- *daub the wall of the* **jakes** *with him* = use him to paint the walls of an outdoor toilet

....

☞ PROSE / POETRY

Halfway through the scene, Kent switches up to verse to talk to Cornwall, and then becomes incredibly poetic with *the wreath of radiant fire / On flickering Phoebus' front*. He switches back to prose to make his point, saying he has gone *out of his dialect* to show he can use flowery speech but chooses not to. It's a risk – Kent is talking to people that knew him before he was banished, and his disguise might be seen through.

....

☞ WORDS

- *i'th'* **mire** = in the swamp / mud
- *None of these rogues and cowards / But* **Ajax** *is their fool* = in classical mythology, Ajax was known for his strength and size, but went mad and killed himself when he wasn't given the armour of dead Achilles
- *a fellow of the self-same* **colour** = type, nature
- *Goose, if I had you upon* **Sarum Plain** */ I'd drive ye cackling home to* **Camelot** = Sarum Plain was a name for Salisbury Plain, the place where the legendary King Arthur fought his last battle and was mortally wounded; Camelot was Arthur's castle (note the Fool's later mention of Merlin in 3:5; also see AFTER p.91); Kent is saying that even if Oswald were King Arthur he'd kill him

💬 SPEECH KENT

14 lines; 6 thoughts, 3 end mid-line. Metrically fairly regular, Kent takes the opportunity of being stocked to read his secret letter from Cordelia – letting the audience discover he has been in contact with her – and to try to rest. His final hope: that the goddess Fortune may look favourably on his cause (see AFTER, p.93).

KENT
Good King, that must approve the common **saw**,
Thou out of Heaven's **benediction** comest
To <u>the warm sun.</u> (x \ x \ x \ )
Approach, thou beacon to this under globe,
That by thy comfortable beams I may
<u>Peruse this letter.</u> Nothing almost sees miracles   **+3**
<u>But misery.</u> I know 'tis from Cordelia,   **+1**
Who hath most fortunately been informed
Of my **obscurèd course**, and '**shall find time**
From this enormous state, seeking to give
<u>Losses their remedies.</u>' All weary and **o'erwatched**,   **+1**
Take vantage, heavy eyes, not to behold
<u>This shameful lodging.</u> (x \ x \ x)
Fortune, good night: smile once more; <u>turn thy wheel.</u>

(He sleeps)

saw = wise saying, maxim

benediction = blessing; come from good to bad

\ x – as Kent takes out Cordelia's letter?

obscured course = disguised way

shall find time... remedies – Kent begins to read the letter aloud

o'erwatched = tired from lack of sleep

\ x – as he replaces the letter? or stretches as best he can?

Act 2:3

(part of 2:2 in Arden edition)

Location: *Somewhere in the countryside*

Characters: *Edgar*

Action: *Having been chased and hunted out of the towns, Edgar tells the audience that his only course of action and escape is to disguise himself as a beggarman.*

The speech is sometimes included as part of the previous scene, although the location is very likely not anywhere near Gloucester's castle – from what he says, it seems Edgar has run far away. As a separate scene with a shift of location, it more easily allows a passage of time for Kent to sleep, for the mood and theme to shift to Edgar and away again. That said, Gloucester's servants seem to know of Tom's whereabouts at the end of 3:7, and as Lear and his train meet Tom soon after leaving Gloucester's castle in 3:4, it could be argued that Edgar hasn't been able to put too much distance between himself and his pursuers.

⬭ SPEECH   EDGAR

21 lines; 5 thoughts, no questions. It opens with a short metrical line, and the thoughts end mid-line until he decides on his course of action. There are slightly longer lines towards the end of the speech, perhaps as he becomes aware of the full horror of his idea, before ending with the final 'Edgar I nothing am' as he gives up everything in life – beginning with his very character – he has known until this point.

The speech is broken into four sections: a call for help; a question of what to do; once decided, a practical thought of how to do it; and an argument of why the plan is a good one.

EDGAR

I heard myself **proclaimed**, (\ x \ x)   -4
And by the **happy** hollow of a tree
Escaped <u>the hunt</u>. No port is free, no place
That guard and most unusual vigilance
Does not attend <u>my taking</u>. Whiles I may 'scape   +1
I will preserve myself; and am bethought
To take the basest and most poorest shape   +1
That e'er **penury**, in contempt of man,
Brought <u>near to beast</u>. My face I'll grime with filth,
Blanket my loins, elf all my hair in knots,
And with presented nakedness **outface**
The winds and persecutions <u>of the sky</u>.
The country gives me proof and precedent
Of **Bedlam** beggars, who, with roaring voices,   +1
Strike in their numbed and **mortified** bare arms
Pins, wooden pricks, nails, sprigs of rosemary;
And with this horrible object, from **low** farms,   +1
Poor pelting villages, **sheepcotes**, and mills
Sometimes with lunatic **bans**, sometime with prayers, +1
Enforce their charity: ' Poor **Turlygod**! Poor Tom,' +2
That's something yet: Edgar <u>I nothing am.</u>

proclaimed – his name declared as an outlaw

\ x – as he gasps for breath? moves to hide? takes in the news of his proclamation?

happy = opportune

penury = poverty

outface = defy

Bedlam = Bethlehem Hospital for the insane, in London

mortified = dead to feeling

low = humble

sheepcote = shelter for sheep

bans = curses

Turlygod, Tom – Edgar tries different names for his beggar character

Act 2:4

(part of 2:2 in Arden edition)

Location: *The grounds of Gloucester's Castle*

Characters: *Kent, Lear, Fool, Gentleman, Cornwall, Regan, Gloucester, Servants, Oswald, Goneril*

Action: *Lear arrives to discover Kent is stocked. He argues with Cornwall and Regan, and is shocked to see Goneril arrive and the two sisters joining together. He leaves angrily, into the coming night and storm.*

Note that Goneril arrives without Albany, a silent nod that the couple are already beginning to go their separate ways. Note, too, that as Lear tells Regan she shall never have his curse, he switches to the more intimate thou.

....

☞ VERSE vs PROSE

The scene opens in verse, then later moves into a fast prose exchange (see below). Before it does there's a nice opening gap in the metre:

GENTLEMAN

10   The night before there was no purpose in them

1–4   Of this remove.

KENT

5–10   Hail to thee, noble master!

LEAR

1 (2–10) Ha! (x \ x \ x \ x \ x)

1-7   Makest thou this shame thy **pastime**?

x \ – as Lear reacts to his stocked servant?

pastime *= hobby*

KENT

8–10   No, my lord.

💬 SPEECH   KENT and LEAR

The interaction between Kent and Lear in the opening of this scene is lovely, funny-tragic writing. Reminiscent of their argument in I:I, Lear can't believe someone would commit such an act against the King, particularly someone so close to him:

LEAR

Where's he that hath so much thy place mistook

To set thee here?

KENT

        It is both he and she;

Your son and daughter.

(switching to Prose)

LEAR No.

KENT Yes.
LEAR No, I say.
KENT I say yea.
LEAR No, no, they would not.
KENT Yes, they have.

With a certain amount of finality, Kent's *Yes, they have* can be a very comic line.

LEAR By Jupiter, I swear no!
KENT By Juno, I swear ay.

Then, after he swears by Jupiter, the Leader of the Gods, and Kent balances the oath swearing by Jupiter's wife Juno, the Queen of the Gods, Lear switches back up to verse:

LEAR
                    They durst not do't;
They could not, would not do't, 'tis worse than murder
To do upon respect such violent outrage.

Lear's later *Follow me not* = stay here – again is sometimes a comic line, if the stocked Kent is included in the instruction. Kent's *Where learned you this, Fool?* and the Fool's reply *Not i'the stocks, fool* allows for another potentially humorous moment, before the coming argument.

· ·

☞ CHARACTER LEAR'S FOLLOWERS

Once Lear has exited, Kent asks

KENT
How chance the King comes with so small a number?

The Fool explains, and says

FOOL
Let go thy hold, when a great wheel runs down a hill,
lest it break thy neck with following

In other words, that Lear's Knights understand the futility of following an increasingly powerless man.

Regan's line towards the end of the scene, that Lear is *attended with a desperate train* (that his followers are careless) harks back to the accusation in 1:4 that Lear's Knights are *riotous* – misbehaving in some way. But it also allows for the idea that those that still follow him are ragged and few, clinging onto the end of something that is dying.

💬 SPEECH   LEAR

23 lines; 11 thoughts, 4 mid-line, 2 gaps in the metre. Longer thoughts in the middle section as Lear's emotions run cooler, bookended by shorter, more emotional thoughts.

I clearly remember studying this speech in school as it begins with one of the play's most powerful lines. Regan and Goneril push Lear back and forth between them, haggling him down to no followers. What kind of King is he without a train? Regan's cue-line for Lear's speech – *What need one?* – runs fast with her sister's argument, adding to its impact.

Earlier in the scene, Lear has mockingly begged forgiveness, even falling to his knees (a King would never kneel to someone else) – an action that should shock all those else present.

Lear's language becomes that of a child; Regan and Goneril quibble with him, like parents telling a child what he does and does not need. And then, a banished boy, he leaves. But his point is true – that the question of *need* is irrelevant:

LEAR

O, **reason** <u>not the need!</u> Our basest beggars   +1
Are in the <u>poorest thing</u> **superfluous.**
Allow not nature more than nature needs –
Man's life is <u>cheap as beast's.</u> Thou art a lady;   +1
If only to **go warm** were gorgeous, (x)   -1
Why, nature needs not what thou gorgeous wear'st,
Which scarcely <u>keeps thee warm.</u> But for true need, –
You heavens, give me that patience, <u>patience I need!</u>   +2
You see me here, you **gods**, a poor old man,
As full of grief as age, wretched in both;
If it be you that stirs these daughters' hearts
Against their father, fool me not so much

reason not = don't argue, or debate the notion of needing something

superfluous – beggars have more than they actually, really need

go warm = be naked

x – gap as he takes a moment to think?

you gods – see AFTER (p.91)

To bear it tamely; touch me with noble anger,   **+2**
And let not women's weapons, water drops,
Stain <u>my man's cheeks</u>! No, you **unnat'ral hags,**
I will have such revenges on you both
That all the world shall – I will do such things –
What they are yet I know not; but they shall be
The terrors <u>of the earth</u>. You <u>think I'll weep.</u>
No, <u>I'll not weep.</u> (x \ x \ x   \)   **-6**
I have full cause of weeping;
(storm and tempest)
                    but this heart
Shall break into a hundred thousand flaws
Or <u>ere I'll weep.</u> O Fool, I <u>shall go mad!</u>

unnat'ral hags = like witches

x \ – as Lear tries to gain control of his emotions?

....

☞ WORDS

- *summoned up their* **meiny** = followers
- **Hysterica passio**, *down* = Latin, for *hysteria*; Lear tries to calm himself as he becomes hysterical
- *mere* **fetches** = dodges, strategy to avoid him
- *now* **presently** = immediately
- *'twas her brother that in pure kindness to his horse* **buttered his hay** = trying to be kind, the brother spreads butter on his horse's hay; in fact, butter was used to stop horses eating
- *I would divorce me from thy mother's tomb /* **Sepulchring** *an adult'ress* = serve as a burial place; Lear says that if Regan were not glad to see him, he would claim that his dead wife committed adultery, that she was not his daughter
- *vouchsafe me* **raiment** = provide me with clothing
- *slave and* **sumpter** = a pack-horse, fit only for carrying heavy goods, not for fast riding
- *high-judging* **Jove** = another name for Jupiter, the Roman supreme god, associated with the heavens and the weather, especially thunder and lightning; Lear's reference to Jove comes immediately before he calls on the storm (in 3:2)
- *he is attended with a* **desperate** *train* = Lear's followers have started to despair
- *what* **trumpet's** *that?* = see *tuckets* (BEFORE, p.24)

Act 3:1

Location: *Somewhere in the countryside*

Characters: *Kent, Gentleman*

Action: *As the storm grows, Kent meets a Gentleman, confirms the division between Cornwall and Albany, gives him news of Cordelia's French powers arriving in England, and asks him to head to Dover, on the English coast. Keeping his disguise, wanting to prove his worth and word, Kent gives the Gentleman a ring to show Cordelia, implying it will establish his identity with her.*

The poetic imagery Shakespeare uses ramps up, and the next few scenes are very rich in their writing style, as the storm builds and Lear's madness and situation reach a desperate climax.

💬 SPEECH GENTLEMAN

A 12-line speech; 2 thoughts, none ending mid-line. Metrically regular, apart from when he talks of Lear trying to out-storm the wind and rain, a horrible sight that must have affected the Gentleman deeply. For a nameless character, he is given an incredibly vivid speech; by removing any association of a person's name or history, the imagery is allowed to blossom more.

As he knows the people involved, it makes a certain sense that Kent makes the speech about the coming wars. In contrast to the Gentleman's speech, his is not just report, he has a personal connection to events. In classical Greek theatre, the speeches would have been the other way around: a nameless messenger would report the news from abroad and Kent, with his direct relationship, would tell of Lear.

KENT
I know you. Where's the King?

GENTLEMAN
Contending with the fretful elements:
Bids the wind blow the earth into the sea,
Or swell the curlèd waters 'bove the main,
That things might change or cease; tears his white hair,
Which the impetuous blasts with eyeless rage
Catch in their fury and make nothing of:
Strives in his little world of man to out-storm   +1
The to-and-fro conflicting <u>wind and rain</u>.
This night, wherein the **cub-drawn** bear would **couch**,
The lion and the **belly-pinchèd** wolf
Keep their fur dry, unbonneted he runs
And bids <u>what will take all.</u>

contending = fighting

Strives... rain – a beautiful image of Lear ranting at the storm, shortly before we get to see it (in 3:2)

cub-drawn = drained of milk by her cubs

couch = find shelter

belly-pinchèd = hungry

....

👉 WORDS

• *in **snuffs** and **packings** of the Dukes* = resentments and plotting
• *he that first **lights** on him / **Holla** the other* = the first person that sees, call 'holla' to the other

Act 3:2

Location: *Somewhere in the countryside*

Characters: *Lear, Fool, Kent*

Action: *The play cranks up a gear, as Lear, bereft of most of his followers, thinking himself betrayed by his daughters, helped by Gloucester and followed only by the Fool and Kent, loses more of his mind as the storm builds and breaks.*

As Lear's wits begin to turn, he becomes more concerned about the Fool's well-being; his attention finally turning away from himself to an awareness of the plight of those around him. This new side to his character doesn't completely hold sway, though: his line I am a man / More sinned against that sinning is brimming with pathos.

○ SPEECH LEAR

The most famous speech in the play, and one of the best-known in the canon. Remarkably metrically regular, aside from the references to his daughters, although including a number of mid-line endings; it perhaps gives the impression of Lear being strangely calm at the eye of the storm:

LEAR
Blow, winds, and crack <u>your cheeks!</u> (x \)Rage, blow! -2
You **cataracts** and hurricanoes, spout
Till you have drenched our steeples, <u>drowned the cocks!</u>
You sulph'rous and thought-executing fires,
Vaunt-curriers of oak-cleaving thunderbolts,
Singe <u>my white head!</u> And thou all-shaking thunder, +1
Smite flat the thick rotundity o'th' world,
Crack Nature's moulds, all **germens spill** at once
That makes <u>ingrateful man!</u> (x \   x \) -4

[Fool interjects...]

Rumble <u>thy bellyful!</u> Spit, fire, <u>spout, rain!</u>
Nor rain, wind, thunder, fire, <u>are my daughters.</u> +1
I tax not you, you elements, with unkindness; +2
I never gave you kingdom, called <u>you children.</u> +1
You owe me no **subscription**; then let fall
Your <u>horrible pleasure.</u> Here I stand, your slave, +1
A poor, infirm, weak, and <u>despised old man.</u>
But yet I call you **servile ministers**,
That will with two **pernicious** daughters join
Your high-engendered battles 'gainst a head
So old and <u>white as this.</u> O, ho! 'Tis foul!

x \ – as thunder claps? or Lear takes breath?
cataracts = downpour or deluge of water
vaunt-curriers = announcers

germens = life-forming elements
spill = destroy
x \ – as Lear's energy flags?

subscription = allegiance

servile ministers = cringing messengers
pernicious = evil, wicked

....

☞ CHARACTER THE FOOL

As Lear is led to the hovel, the Fool sings a song:

FOOL
He that has and a little tiny wit,
With heigh-ho, the wind and the rain,
Must make content with his fortunes fit,
Though the rain it raineth every day.

This verse is very similar to a song another Fool, Feste, sings to close the play *Twelfth Night*, written a few years earlier. Shakespeare's audience might well remember this echoing refrain. It is often played comically in *Twelfth Night*, though has a more solemn undertone here, as the Fool watches his King unravel.

See AFTER (p.91) for a look at the prophecy – referencing Merlin and Albion – that the Fool gives before he exits.

☞ WORDS

- **Caitiff**, *to pieces shake* = a miserable creature
- *this dreadful* **pudder** = din, roar
- **close** *pent-up guilts* = **secret**
- **rive** *your concealing continents* = **burst from**
- **cry** / *These dreadful summoners grace* = **beg** good will; a **summoner** was a court-officer, who ensured attendance at a hearing
- *here is a* **hovel** = a small, humble shelter, or very wretched house; originally, the tiring-house, behind a central, upstage door at Shakespeare's Globe

Act 3:3

Location: *Inside Gloucester's Castle*

Characters: *Gloucester, Edmund*

Action: *Gloucester, unhappy with what has happened to Lear but unaware of Edmund's intended betrayal, tells his half-son he will try to help Lear in whatever way he can, come what may…*

The factions divide. Gloucester is in receipt of letters from Cordelia and France, intending to help restore the King to power. Edmund intends to help Cornwall, and betray his father.

The father-son exchange stays in prose until Gloucester leaves, then Edmund switches up into poetry – perhaps a sign of his growing sense of self and social standing? He ends the scene with a rhyming couplet, and his final The younger rises when the old doth fall *echoes the Fortune's wheel theme that has been sounding throughout the play.*

☞ WORDS

- *I have locked the letter in my **closet*** = a cabinet, or private room
- *There is part of a **power** already **footed*** = an **army** already **landed** in the country; Cordelia has secretly invaded with French troops
- *There is strange things **toward*** = impending, forthcoming
- *This courtesy **forbid** thee shall the Duke / Instantly know* = the courtesy of helping Lear, which you were forbidden to do, shall the Duke of Cornwall instantly hear of

Act 3:4

Location: *Somewhere in the countryside*

Characters: *Lear, Fool, Kent, Edgar (disguised as Poor Tom now until halfway through 4:6), Gloucester*

Action: *As the storm continues to rage and the King's mind to unravel, Kent leads Lear to a shelter, where they encounter a mad, half-naked beggarman who Lear becomes fascinated with. Gloucester arrives, having found a safe and warm place for Lear to rest.*

There's almost a tug-of-war in the scene as the Fool's speeches become more and more sensible but fall on deaf ears, while Poor Tom's mad rambling enchants Lear.

Here the Lear plot and Edgar sub-plot, having darted around each other, meet for the first time. They remain fused, coming apart again only for short scenes between Lear and Cordelia; and Edgar and Gloucester.

☞ CHARACTER POOR TOM

A closer look at Edgar's choice of disguise and the character of Poor Tom is in AFTER (p.94), but the main things to know are:

• Tom was once a serving man, but he committed all of the seven deadly sins – pride, gluttony, lust, greed, sloth, wrath, and envy – and drank, gambled and betrayed all around him
• Apparently then he hit penury, went mad and is now convinced he is being chased by a devil
• We hear him call the thing chasing him the *foul fiend*, *Flibberdigibbet*, *Modo*, *Mahu*, and *Smulkin*

The image – of a fallen nobleman, chased by a devil – without Edgar knowing it, echoes his own situation. For him, the chasing sprite is very real: his brother Edmund.

An interesting staging point – when Gloucester later arrives, how does Edgar / Poor Tom react to seeing his father – aside from calling him by the devil's name, saying *This is the foul fiend Flibberdigibbet*? And will Gloucester see through his disguise?

He ends the scene with a dark reference to two fairytales – *Childe Rowland and the Dark Tower*, and *Jack and the Beanstalk*.

Childe Rowland sees three brothers, one-by-one, try to rescue their sister from a dark tower inhabited by the Faery King. The third brother succeeds having been armed with Excalibur by Merlin. The phrase *Fie foh fum* comes from the Jack the Giant-slayer stories.

> **EDGAR**
> Childe Roland to the dark tower came
> His word was still 'fie, foh and fum
> I smell the blood of a British man'.

The antiquated allusions aside, these last few lines are a sinister presage of the bloody scene about to take place in Gloucester's own dark tower…

The Arden edition follows the First Folio, and has the spelling *childe* – a medieval term not for a young human, but for an untested Knight (perhaps an Arthurian Knight?), as Edgar indeed is.

☞ CHARACTER LEAR

Lear switches down to prose when he meets Poor Tom. An unusual action for a King, though considering the situation, Lear's state of mind and Tom's apparent inability to switch up to verse, it makes a certain sense. If circumstance and social standing are 'clothes' (i.e. accidents of Fate or Fortune, and thereby essentially meaningless) it follows that Lear treats a beggar as an equal. Indeed, at this point he treats everyone as equals – as long as they refrain from the disguises of 'civilisation'.

Seeing Tom's wretchedness, Lear pulls his clothes off. Some productions have had Lear become completely naked, others merely down to his underclothes. Whichever choice is made, naked in a storm, with a Fool and a vagrant madman for company, this is as far from King as Lear can be.

Apparently seeing Tom as a symbol of his country and his people, and in the only reference to his time as monarch preceding the play, Lear says *O, I have ta'en / Too little care of this*. With still more care for his Fool, his emerging awareness is perhaps best elicited in his next line: *Take physic, pomp* (take medicine, greatness) – a self-castigating note, to shift away from luxury in the face of others' poverty.

☞ WORDS

• ***S'withold*** *footed thrice the 'old* = **Saint Withold** (a defender against harms) walked around the **wold** (= open, hilly countryside) three times; three was considered a magic number, and perhaps Poor Tom uses this rhyme to ward off the demons tormenting him
• *the **cat** no perfume* = the civet cat was a source of perfume
• *'tis a **naughty** night to swim in* = it's a horrible night to play around in
• *he gives **the web and the pin*** = a disease of the eye, similar to a cataract, that obscures sight
• *this same learned **Theban*** = Thebes was the city of wisdom and learning; in his madness, Lear sees the beggar Poor Tom as being learned; later calling him a *good Athenian* – Athens was the cradle of Western civilisation and democracy

Act 3:5

Location: *Inside Gloucester's Castle*

Characters: *Edmund, Cornwall*

Action: *Edmund, pretending to be conflicted at betraying his father, betrays his father, giving Cornwall Gloucester's letter from Cordelia. Cornwall vows revenge, and promises to give Gloucester's title to Edmund.*

A short scene, that has been been played in different ways. How aware of Edmund's duplicitousness is Cornwall? How much of Edmund's earnest 'I am good, I'm so sorry to have to betray my father' does Cornwall believe? The scene has been played that both are aware of Edmund's machinations, and Cornwall plays along.

Cornwall's second line is slightly tricky:

CORNWALL
I now perceive it was not altogether your brother's evil disposition made him seek his death; but a provoking merit set a-work by a reprovable badness in himself.

It essentially runs

I understand now that Edgar's evil nature wasn't the sole reason for seeking Gloucester's death; Gloucester's treachery in spying for France set the already-evil nature in Edgar to work.

The end point is that Edmund is made Earl of Gloucester by Cornwall – he has got what he set out to get. Now where is there left for him to go? Ever upward, and although the idea isn't written into the play but is left to us to divine, Edmund could try to partner up with Regan or Goneril, which would gain him further power and a line to the throne…

....

☞ WORDS

- *I may be **censured*** = I may be condemned
- *I must repent to be **just*** = I must repent that I am honourable / loyal to the State

Act 3:6

> **Location:** *A barn, or some other warm shelter from the storm*
>
> **Characters:** *Gloucester, Kent, Edgar, Fool, Lear*
>
> **Action:** *Brought by Gloucester to a place where he can rest, Lear comes to the height of his madness and puts an imaginary Regan and Goneril on trial. He eventually sleeps, and Gloucester tells Kent he has arranged transport for them all to Dover, where Cordelia awaits.*
>
> *In stage productions, the interval often comes at the end of this scene, using the Fool's departure and Edgar's relinquishing of his disguise as a fitting end to the first half.*

....

☞ CHARACTER   THE FOOL

This is the last time we see the Fool. Dramatically, his function is made redundant; in the depths of his madness, Lear can no longer hear the counsel the Fool offers, refusing to listen to anyone but Poor Tom, his *learned philosopher*. The Fool's lines are clearer to understand here than perhaps anywhere else, and follow a thread of sense while Tom seems to encourage Lear's madness and hallucinations.

Productions have had the Fool grow increasingly ill, have had him linger at the end of the scene and be caught and killed by Cornwall's soldiers, or have tried to reintroduce the character at the end. Shakespeare, it is generally argued, used the character until there was nothing to be gained from having him present, and then simply forgot to write him out.

....

☞ THE TRIAL OF GONERIL AND REGAN

At the height of Lear's dark, frenzied night madness, he sets up the Fool, Poor Tom and Kent as Judges, and using furniture in the hovel to stand for Regan and Goneril, puts his daughters on trial for their awful treatment of him. He sees one of his 'children' try to escape, and then 'dogs' bark at him. He wants to see Regan *anatomised* – openly dissected in front of him. In one of many apparently lucid moments, he asks, bemused at his daughters' treatment of him, *Is there any cause in nature that makes these hard hearts?* It's a terrifying, pitiable moment.

This hovel-courtroom moment is the climax of this run of scenes, which begins with the scene ending with the *O reason not the need* speech, traverses the storm scene and the meeting with Tom, to meet this parody of justice.

Shakespeare kindly gives Lear an on-stage opportunity to rest, before being carried away. The normal 4th Act break is included for the actor too, and it's not until 4:6 we see a calmer, softer Lear return, his madness switched into a different gear.

....

☞ CHARACTER EDGAR

Edgar, seeing how burdened the King has become, gains some perspective on his own problems, and ends the scene with a rhyming soliloquy: *When we our betters see bearing our woes / We scarcely think our miseries our foes…*

His simple *He childed as I fathered* sums up the play to this point perfectly – Lear whose children seek his life, Edgar whose father seeks his life. He decides to shed his Poor Tom disguise, choosing to stay out of sight (*Lurk, lurk*) until he finds an opportunity to deal with his misfortune in a more active way…

....

☞ WORDS

- *whether a madman be a gentleman or a* **yeoman** = a land-holding farmer, but not a gentleman (i.e. not of the nobility)
- *I will* **arraign** *them* **straight** = put on trial immediately
- *Thou* **sapient** *sir* = wise, learned
- *his* **yoke-fellow** *of* **equity** = his comrade in fairness
- *one blast of they* **minikin** *mouth* = shrill, high-pitched
- **avaunt**, *you curs!* = begone
- *thy* **horn** *is dry* = drinking-horn
- *let them* **anatomise** *Regan* = dissect, lay open; a hideous image, especially for the time Shakespeare was writing, when public dissections of human bodies were becoming popular excursions

Act 3:7

Location: *Gloucester's Castle*

Characters: *Cornwall, Regan, Goneril, Edmund, Servants, Oswald, Gloucester*

Action: *Sending Goneril and Edmund to advise Albany of the invading French army, Cornwall takes control of Gloucester's Castle. He orders servants to find Gloucester, and there follows one of the most gruesome scenes in the canon.*

There's an opportunity at the top of the scene for Edmund and Goneril, or Edmund and Regan, or both, to briefly show the beginnings of their developing relationship(s). We'll hear more of those in a few scenes' time.

....

☞ GLOUCESTER'S BLINDING

There are few scenes in Shakespeare as horrific as the torture Gloucester endures at the hands of Regan and Cornwall.

Gloucester's shock when Regan plucks his beard is justified – beards were thought of as a mark of wisdom, and should have inspired respect. A lovely run of shared lines follows, allowing Gloucester a pause before he gives up the truth:

GLOUCESTER
10   I have a letter guessingly set down
10   Which came from one that's of a neutral heart
1–6   And not from one opposed.

CORNWALL
7–8   Cunning.

REGAN
9–10   And false.

CORNWALL
1–6   Where has thou sent the King?

GLOUCESTER
(7), 8–10   (x) To Dover.

His blinding is made worse by the interval between the plucking out of each eye, some dozen lines or so of dialogue. Cornwall's line *Out, vile jelly!* is deliciously sick-making, and vivid enough, though most productions enhance the horror by using as much blood as can be squeezed from the actor's hands. The substance used for the eyes, which are usually hurled to the floor, varies – many productions opt for a material that squelches as well as bounces.

Only once he is blinded does Gloucester 'see' the truth, learning from Regan of Edmund's treachery, and his abuse of Edgar.

....

☞ WORDS

- *a most **festinate** preparation* = speedy
- ***Hot questrists** after him* = eager seekers
- ***naughty** lady* = meaning wicked, rather than the modern sexual connotation
- *get the **Bedlam** / To lead him* = the beggarman; the implication being that Poor Tom is somehow known to be nearby

Act 4:1

Location: *Somewhere in the countryside*

Characters: *Edgar, Old Man, Gloucester*

Action: *While Lear takes a rest, we move forward with the Gloucester subplot. Edgar, no longer in hiding, but keeping his Poor Tom disguise, is reunited with his now blinded father, and promises to lead Gloucester to a clifftop in Dover.*

One disguised, still hunted, and miserable: the other blind, suicidal, and with the son he longs to be forgiven by, they make for a beautifully tragic pair.

65

☞ **CHARACTER** GLOUCESTER

Blinded, but now seeing the truth behind Edmund's lies, Gloucester takes on a Lear-like quality in his speeches. Up to this point, he's often spoken in prose or barely at all: but now his lines become beautiful.

Two in particular, in this scene, stick in the mind:

> **GLOUCESTER**
> As flies to wanton boys are we to the gods;
> They kill us for their sport

He echoes a character from a very early Shakespeare play, *Titus Andronicus*. Titus, at the depths of his sorrow and flitting into madness, berates his brother for killing a fly. Gloucester has blamed the stars, nature, and now the gods themselves, as we all do when in the pits of despair.

He's being led by one of his servants, who protests at Gloucester's desire to let the beggarman Poor Tom lead him on. The second line comes:

> **GLOUCESTER**
> Tis the time's plague, when madmen lead the blind.

The pair become a symbol of the state of Lear's lost kingdom, now in such ruin that only madmen can help lead the sightless.

☞ **CHARACTER** EDGAR

As Edgar realises he must press on with the charade of Poor Tom – not knowing his father has discovered he is innocent – he continues to take us, the audience, into his confidence, and flips in and out of character, allowing us to hear what he's thinking. After the shattering sight of his blind father – *World, world, O world* – he manages to carry on pretending, showing terrific strength.

His speech at the beginning of the scene has a hearty, zen-like acceptance of his state, bringing back the theme of Fortune, but for the first time taking a positive spin – *To be worst… stands still in esperence, lives not in fear* – even at the very worst, there is still hope.

He thinks he has got as low he can get – but as he is about to see, with the arrival of his father, it is all about to get much, much worse.

☞ WORDS

- *stands still in* **esperence** = always lives in hope
- *My father,* **parti-eyed** = with eyes of mixed colours; bleeding
- *That slaves your* **ordinance** = that brings divine rule into subjection (that can even overrule a god-like power)

Act 4:2

> **Location:** *Albany's Castle*
>
> **Characters:** *Goneril, Edmund, Oswald, Albany, Messenger*
>
> **Action:** *Arriving at her castle, Goneril discovers Albany has aligned himself with Lear. She decides to take charge, sends Edmund back to Cornwall's castle, but not before secretly giving him a favour (very often a jewel or chain) to wear and a kiss. As both sisters begin to show interest in Edmund, the plot and subplot continue to intertwine.*

☞ CHARACTER ALBANY

The Duke of Albany is one of those Shakespeare characters that you can do a lot or a little with, depending on how well he's cast. He has very few scenes, spread out across the play, and relatively few lines. Dominated by Goneril, her line *A fool usurps my bed* gives us a rather negative impression before we see him, although it is well-balanced by Oswald's report of him: *never man so changed*. It's easy to pigeonhole Albany into the same Evil box as his wife, her sister and her sister's husband.

This scene is the turning point for him, no matter how murky his prior motivations. It's refreshing to see him stand his ground – *thou changed and self-covered thing* (= self-concealing thing) – in what becomes a bitter row with Goneril: and as the Messenger arrives with news of Cornwall's death, Gloucester's blinding and Edmund's betrayal, a much-needed shot in the arm for Good to hear Albany vowing to revenge Gloucester's blinding.

His support of Lear and Gloucester does not bode entirely well – before Cornwall was killed, Albany was at the beginnings of war with him, and the kingdom is nearly leaderless, lying open to the invading French army. He may endorse Lear's cause, but invasion is still invasion.

....

☞ SIDE-NOTE   THE DUKE OF GLOUCESTER

As Goneril and Edmund part, she bids him goodbye with a new title:

EDMUND
Yours, in the ranks of death.

GONERIL
                              My most dear Gloucester!

It's the first time Edmund has been called by this title. His father is now essentially considered dead and gone. With his new social standing, he has inherited the dukedom, and is the Duke of Gloucester.

....

☞ WORDS

- *It is the* **cowish** *terror of his spirit* = cowardly
- *hasten his* **musters** = an enlistment of soldiers
- *give the* **distaff** / *Into my husband's hands* = a device for weaving; Goneril uses it as a metaphor for the person who is wielding the power
- **sliver** *and* **disbranch** / *From her material sap* = split off and sever
- **head-lugged** *bear* = pulled along by the ears

Act 4:3

Location: *Unclear; likely in or near the French Army's Camp, Dover*

Characters: *Kent, Gentleman*

Action: *Another news-reporting/messenger scene, which is often cut from productions. To explain why Cordelia is leading the invasion, we hear the King of France has returned home. Dramatically, it puts the strong-willed Cordelia in charge; functionally, it frees up the actor who played France in the first scene to play a different role.*

....

☞ CHARACTERS KENT, GENTLEMAN, AND CORDELIA

We hear of Cordelia before we see her; our last sight of her was a strong, defiant, banished daughter; the image we now have painted for us is of a beautiful, grieving Queen longing to right her father's wrongs, saddened by what has taken place since she left for France. When her reaction to Kent's letters is recounted, the scene shifts from prose into verse, and once more the Gentleman character is given rich, poetic language:

GENTLEMAN
> You have seen
> Sunshine and rain at once; her smile and tears
> Were like a better way; those happy smilets
> That played on her ripe lip seemed not to know
> What guests were in her eyes, which parted thence
> As pearls from diamond dropped.

For what is essentially an expositional scene, the verse –while pretty – is given pace as Kent and the Gentleman's remaining dialogue is all in shared lines.

Kent's *It is the stars, / The stars above us govern our conditions,* echoes the earlier superstitious intonation of Gloucester; unusual words for a man who hitherto has been relentlessly practical. One of the wonderful things about this play: and every character in this play shifts, as people do, showing an unexpected side just as you think you know who they are.

....

WORDS

- *her **ripe** lip* = red and full, like ripe fruit
- ***mate** and **make*** = husband and wife
- *such different **issues*** = children

Act 4:4

Location: *An army camp, near Dover*
Characters: *Cordelia, Doctor, soldiers*
Action: *The return of Cordelia.*

....

CHARACTER CORDELIA

The first time we see Cordelia since the opening scene of the play. It's tricky to play well: she needs to win our sympathy and get us to buy into the idea that she has become a Joan-of-Arc-style Queen-warrior, leading the French invasion.

....

LEAR'S CROWN

*Crowned with rank **fumiter*** = foul-smelling weed
furrow-weeds = a weed that grows in the furrows of ploughed fields
hardokes = a type of weed (also spelt *burdock*)
darnel = a type of weed

....

WORDS

- *our **foster-nurse** of nature is repose* = a nurse who brings up another's child; sleep heals, an echo of Shakespeare's earlier play *Macbeth*, where madness comes in part from a lack of sleep
- *in him / Are many **simples operative*** = effective medicine
- ***aidant** and **remediate*** = helpful and healing

Act 4:5

Location: *Unclear, but likely to be Regan's castle*

Characters: *Regan, Oswald*

Action: *A letter-centric scene; the main import of the dialogue is twofold:*

- *through Regan, we gain further intimations of Goneril and Edmund's developing relationship, plus the notion that (at least according to her) Edmund has actually already agreed to unite with Regan*
- *Regan, giving Oswald a letter for Edmund, tells the Steward he'll be rewarded if he finds and kills Gloucester*

Regan speaks in verse, but the cowardly Oswald stays in prose until she tells him The ways are dangerous – so when he switches up to the more formal speech-style of verse is this a sign that what she has said has had the desired effect on him?

....

☞ SIDE-NOTE THOU / YOU

Using all the tricks of persuasion at her disposal in an effort to see the letters, productions have had Regan try to seduce Oswald into submission. There's a lovely shift in the way she talks to him too, moving in one speech from the formal *you* to the informal *thou*:

> **REGAN**
> Why should she write to Edmund? Might not *you*
> Transport her **purposes** by word? **Belike,**
> Some things – I know not what – I'll love *thee* much –
> Let me unseal the letter.

purposes = intentions

belike = presumably

....

☞ WORDS

- *strange **oeillades** = looks; pronounced [oy-lads]*
- *I know you are of her **bosom** = in her confidence; although some productions take the sexual implication – that Goneril and Oswald have a deeper relationship*

Act 4:6

Location: *Countryside near Dover*

Characters: *Gloucester, Edgar, Lear, Soldiers, Oswald*

Action: *A long, intricate, and epic scene, beginning with Edgar's well-meaning deception of his father, the return of Lear, and the slaying of the coward Oswald.*

Edgar, having promised to take the suicidal Gloucester to a clifftop, instead takes him to a flat stretch of land. He tells us, perhaps slightly weakly, that he hopes surviving a suicide attempt might heal his fathers' misery: Why I do trifle thus with his despair / Is done to cure it.

Gloucester 'jumps', and Edgar takes on a new character, that of a sailor who saw Gloucester 'fall'.

The two fathers, abused by their children, finally meet. One blinded, the other maddened.

Cordelia's soldiers arrive to bring Lear to safety, but he thinks they will capture him, tricks them and runs away. As Edgar and Gloucester make to leave, they encounter Oswald, bearing letters from Goneril to Edmund, and looking to gain a reward for killing Gloucester.

Edgar kills Oswald, who in his dying breath asks for letters to be taken to Edmund. Edgar reads them and learns of Goneril's plot against her husband Albany…

🔖 CHARACTER EDGAR / POOR TOM / SAILOR

The suicidal moment at the 'clifftop' can be tricky to conceive if you're new to the play, and is discussed earlier (BEFORE, p.9). Whether the audience buys into the moment is dependent on Edgar's skill at conjuring up the 'view' down to the sea, and his quick-change into the sailor who saw Gloucester 'fall'.

His shifting personas made slightly less clear as he uses the term of respect (*father* = old man) to a man who is of course his actual father.

It's fascinating to hear Edgar's description of Poor Tom leaving Gloucester at the cliff-edge – his own vision of his beggarman/serving man chased by the devil is horrifying:

EDGAR
Upon the crown o'th cliff what thing was that
Which parted from you?

GLOUCESTER
                            A poor unfortunate beggar.

EDGAR
As I stood here below methought his eyes
Were two full moons; he had a thousand noses
Horns **welked** and waved like the **enridged** sea.
It was some fiend. Therefore, thou **happy** father,
Think that the **clearest** gods, who **make them honours**
Of men's impossibilities, have preserved thee.

welked = twisted
enridged = rippling
happy = lucky
clearest = faultless
make them honours...
– the gods gain honour by doing the impossible

🔖 SIDE-NOTE STAGE DIRECTION

Enter Lear, fantastically dressed with wild flowers

Shakespeare is famous for having very few explicit stage directions, and so the few that exist stand out. One of the most famous in the canon, this reintroduction of Lear, coming out the other side of his madness, would have been no less shocking than his desperate actions were on the heath and in the hovel. It's worth reflecting back, and appreciating the difference in character from the King we saw in the first scene.

○ SPEECH LEAR

25 lines; 17 thoughts, 3 questions at the beginning, 3 exclamations at the end, a switch in speech style halfway through a thought. Very clearly then, a rather complicated speech, spoken by Lear in his calmer madness.

Beginning in verse, Lear seems to alternate between regular iambic pentameter and iambic trimeter (a line of 6 beats), before switching to prose towards the end.

As he flits from subject to subject, and back and forth between verse styles, a number of metrical gaps are left. I hesitate to suggest what fills the gaps in the metre here. The choices are simply as wide open as any speech I've seen in Shakespeare's works, and entirely dependent on how the actor playing Lear thinks his way through this epic speech, that ends with a stage direction indicating the simplest gesture.

GLOUCESTER
The **trick** of that voice I do well remember.   +1
Is't not the King?

LEAR
          Ay, every <u>inch a king.</u>
When I do stare see how <u>the **subject** quakes.</u>
I pardon <u>that man's life.</u> What <u>was thy cause?</u>
Adultery? (x \ x \ x \)   -6
Thou <u>shalt not die. Die for adultery? No.</u>
The wren goes to't, and the small gilded fly
Does lecher <u>in my sight.</u> (x   \   x   \)   -4
Let copulation thrive; for Gloucester's bastard son   +1
Was kinder to his father than my daughters   +1
Got 'tween <u>the lawful sheets.</u> (x \ x \)   -4
To't, **luxury, pell-mell,** for <u>I lack soldiers.</u>
Behold yon simpering dame (x   \   x   \)   -4
Whose face between her forks presages snow,
That minces virtue and does shake the head
To hear of pleasure's name – (x \ x \)   -4
The **fitchew** nor the soilèd horse goes to't
With a <u>more riotous appetite.</u> (x)   -1

trick = distinguishing trait, idiosyncrasy

subject = person owing allegiance

adultery – never discussed in the play, the implication that Gloucester committed adultery when he father Edmund

luxury = lust, lechery

pell-mell = in disordered haste

fitchew = skunk; also, prostitute

> Down from the waist they are **centaurs,** (x \\)   -2
> Though women all above; (x   \   x   \\)   -4
> But to the **girdle** do the gods inherit,
> Beneath is all the fiends' – (x   \   x   \\)   -4
> There's hell, there's darkness, there is the sulphurous pit
> – burning, scalding, <u>stench, consumption!</u> <u>Fie, fie, fie!</u>
> <u>Pah, pah!</u> Give me an ounce of civet, good **apothecary,**
> <u>sweeten my imagination.</u> There's <u>money for thee.</u>
>
> *He gives flowers*

centaur – *in classical mythology, half-man, half-horse*

girdle = *waist*

apothecary = *one who prepares and sells medicinal drugs*

☞ SIDE-NOTE EDGAR'S LANGUAGE

Now out of his beggarman's rags, Edgar probably looks more like his old self. He seems to forget his disguise a little at the top of the scene:

GLOUCESTER
Me thinks thy voice is altered, and thou speak'st
In better phrase and matter than thou didst.

EDGAR
Y'are much deceived. In nothing am I changed
But in my garments.

GLOUCESTER
Methinks y'are better spoken.

Some productions have it that Gloucester starts to guess at Poor Tom's real identity, others that he simply becomes suspicious of his beggarly helper, and his switch from *thou speaks't* to the formal *you* in *Methinks y'are better spoken* would back that idea up.

Hoping to keep his identity hidden, Edgar's language shifts when Oswald approaches. In so doing, we hear a very rare instance of Shakespeare using a regional accent. From the lack of them throughout the canon, it seems he wasn't interested in the dramatic device of having his characters adopt accents different from their own. The dialect he takes on has elements of the West Country of England to it, and is harder to understand in print than spoken:

- **'chould** *ha bin zwaggered out of my life* = I should have been bullied out of my life
- **che vor' ye** = I warn you
- *your* **costard** *or my* **ballow** *be the harder* = a costard was a type of apple, Edgar asks whether Oswald's head or his stick will be the harder
- *no matter vor your* **foins** = sword-thrusts

....

☞ WORDS

- *yon tall anchoring* **bark** / *Diminished to her* **cock** = the tall anchored ship, seems as small as its lookout post
- *i'th'***clout** = a rag, or piece of cloth
- *there's your* **press-money** = money paid to recruits when they're conscripted
- *That fellow handles his bow like a* **crow-keeper** = a scarecrow
- *I am not* **ague-proof** = immune to sickness
- *the* **fitchew** *nor the soiled horse* = skunk; sometimes prostitute
- *The* **usurer** *hangs the* **cozoner** = the money-lender hangs the fraudster
- **plate** *sins with gold* = cover sins with golden armour
- *an ounce of* **civet** = perfume; obtained from a particular type of cat
- *methinks I hear the beaten* **drum** = drums would be beaten to signal an advancing army

Act 4:7

Location: *The French Army's camp, near Dover*

Characters: *Cordelia, Kent, Doctor, Lear, Gentleman*

Action: *Having been brought to her camp, rested and treated, Lear is finally reunited with Cordelia…*

☞ CHARACTER LEAR

Woken by music from a drug-induced (the *simples operative* mentioned in 4:4) sleep, Lear invokes the image of the wheel of Fortune, turning it into an image of hell, imagining Cordelia to be as dead as he, but blissfully in Heaven:

> **LEAR**
> You do me wrong to take me out o'the grave.
> Thou art a soul in bliss; but I am bound
> Upon a wheel of fire, that mine own tears
> Do scald like molten lead.

And his lines following shortly afterwards are, perhaps, the height of his journey to self-awareness:

> **LEAR**
> I am a very foolish fond old man,
> **Four score and upward**, not an hour more nor less   +1   *four score and upward*
> And, to deal plainly, (x \ x \ x)   -5   *= above 80 years old*
> I fear I am not in my perfect mind.   x \ *– as he finally*
>   *admits the truth?*

He ends his speech:

> **LEAR**
> Methinks I should know you, and know this man; (x)   -1   x *– a moment as he*
> Yet I am doubtful; for I am mainly ignorant   +2   *becomes doubtful?*
> What place this is; and all the skill I have
> Remembers not these garments; nor I know not
> Where I did lodge last night. Do not laugh at me,   +1
> For as I am a man, I think this lady
> To be my child Cordelia.

> **CORDELIA**
> (weeping)
>   And so I am, I am.   +2

These last repeated extra syllables are a point of contention. Some consider them a mistake, others agree that the shared line intentionally extends the metre, Cordelia's emotions fittingly breaking past the confines of the poetic style.

☞ SIDE-NOTE

There's no 'right' way to do Shakespeare, and any production's choices can be worthy. Equally, there's no 'right' way to respond to any part of any Shakespeare play.

That said, if you see *Lear* and this scene doesn't make you cry, then either (a) consider asking for your money back, (b) consider therapy, or (c) both.

Bound with the sound of Cordelia's tears by all rights should be the tinkling of the audience's collective heart.

....

☞ CHARACTERS   KENT AND THE
GENTLEMAN

A moment of rest, quietness, and tears in the play, after the flurry of madness and fighting of the previous few scenes, and before the final scenes of action. The happy-sadness is relieved by Kent's discussion with the Gentleman at the end, with news of the coming war factions, and a moment of humour in the report of Kent and Edgar's whereabouts:

> **GENTLEMAN** Holds it true sir, that the Duke of Cornwall was so slain?
> **KENT** Most certain, sir.
> **GENTLEMAN** Who is conductor of his people?
> **KENT** As 'tis said, the bastard son of Gloucester.
> **GENTLEMAN** They say Edgar, his banished son, is with the Earl of Kent in Germany.
> **KENT** Report is changeable.

....

☞ WORDS

• these **weeds** are memories of those worser hours = clothes (in bad condition); Kent's disguise
• still far **wide** = confused
• **four score** and upward = eighty and above
• to watch, poor **perdu**, with this thin **helm**? = literally, a sentry exposed to danger; helmet
• my **point** and **period** will be thoroughly wrought = both have a meaning towards 'end of life'

Act 5.1

Location: *Near the battlefield*

Characters: *Edmund, Regan, Gentleman, soldiers, Goneril, Albany, Edgar*

Action: *Edmund and Albany prepare for battle, as we see Regan and Goneril fight more openly over Edmund; he ends the scene asking the audience which of the Queens we think he should choose.*

Edgar, on a leap of faith, comes to Albany with the letter he took from Oswald, and with another revealing Edmund's villainy to Gloucester.

....

☞ SIDE-NOTE   DOUBT VS FEAR

A number of words that Shakespeare used have changed their meaning over the centuries. Often, they don't trip the listener up, but in this case it usually does. Regan, having sent Oswald with a letter for Edmund, meets her intended lover and finds him without her message:

> **REGAN**
> Our **sister's man** is certainly **miscarried**.
>
> **EDMUND**
> 'Tis to be **doubted,** madam.

sister's man = Oswald
miscarried = come to harm
doubted = feared

It's incumbent on the skill of the modern Shakespeare actor for Edmund to say the word *doubted* but plainly mean the opposite, that he is agreeing with Regan, it is to be feared that Oswald is dead. The same phrase occurs a few lines later (see WORDS, below).

....

☞ WORDS

• the **forfended** *place* = forbidden; a not especially subtle metaphor for *had sex with*
• *I am* **doubtful** *that you have been* **conjunct** / *And* **bosomed**

with her = I fear you have coupled and been close to her; again, a polite way of asking Edmund if he's slept with Goneril

• *let's then determine with the **ancient** of war on our proceeding* = the **strategies** of war

• *we'll use his **countenance** for the battle* = favourable appearance

Act 5:2

> **Location:** *Near the battlefield*
>
> **Characters:** *Lear, Cordelia, soldiers, Edgar, Gloucester*
>
> **Action:** *This very short scene begins with a cross-over: Lear and Cordelia with their soldiers (the stage direction sweetly says Cordelia is holding Lear's hand), entering, crossing the stage, and exiting. It's purely functional, to show their powers – perhaps an opportunity to remind us that they're inferior to Edmund and Albany's army.*
>
> *The fast dialogue has Edgar safely deposit his blind father by a tree, while he joins the fray. Off-stage we hear the sounds of battle, and the sound of retreat, before Edgar returns with the news that Lear and Cordelia have been captured, and the battle lost.*

....

☞ **SIDE-NOTE** EDGAR's Father

EDGAR
Here, **father**, take the shadow of this tree
For your good **host**. Pray that the right may thrive.
If ever I return to you again
I'll bring you comfort.

GLOUCESTER
                    Grace go with you, sir!

father = used as a term of respect to a stranger, although it's hard for a modern audience to ignore the double-meaning

host = shelter, hospitality

Gloucester's final line in the scene – his last in the play – once Edgar has returned with news that they have lost the battle, is slightly weak, and difficult to play strongly, although he is agreeing with Edgar's positive outlook:

GLOUCESTER
No further, sir; a man may rot even here.

EDGAR
What, in **ill** thoughts again? Men must endure
Their going hence even as their coming hither;
Ripeness is all. Come on.

GLOUCESTER
                    And that's true too.

Exeunt

ill = negative

ripeness = readiness; echoing Hamlet's fifth act line The readiness is all

Some productions have played that something in the line Men must endure… is recognisable in some way. He means that similar to the struggle of birth, death must equally only be allowed to come after an appropriate fight. The exchange can be played to give Gloucester a further hint of Edgar's real identity, thereby allowing the final line to become incredibly powerful.

But then, Shakespeare will withhold from us what we have been yearning for – to actually see Edgar's revelation of his true identity to his father, and their reconciliation.

Act 5:3

Location: *The battlefield*

Characters: *Edmund, Cordelia, Lear, Captain, soldiers, Albany, Goneril, Regan, officers, Herald, Edgar, Gentleman, Kent*

Action: *Having captured Cordelia and Lear, Edmund sends them to prison; then sends a Captain after them with instructions to kill them both.*

*Albany arrives, is angry that Edmund has acted without his permission (*I hold you but a subject of this war / Not as a brother*) and a quarrel between the two sisters breaks out over Edmund. Regan publically proposes to Edmund, but Albany intervenes; having read Edgar's letter, he arrests Edmund for treason.*

Albany challenges Edmund, the Herald's trumpet sounds three times, and a masked Edgar arrives to finally duel with, and take revenge on, his half-brother.

Albany challenges Edmund, the Herald's trumpet sounds three times, and a masked Edgar arrives to finally duel and take revenge on his half-brother.

We hear that Gloucester has died – his heart broke smilingly *when Edgar revealed his true identity; that Goneril has killed herself; and that Regan is poisoned by Goneril. Before Edmund dies, he tries to save the lives of Lear and Cordelia…*

It's a packed final scene, full of revelations, deaths and resolution, and the ending is nothing less than utterly tragic.

🗩 SPEECH KENT AND LEAR

Again, so soon after not getting to see Edgar and Gloucester reconciled, we have another aborted moment of recognition. After Kent has been doggedly, tirelessly following his master, they are finally reunited; our expectation, that Kent might at the least be gratefully acknowledge by his master, is thwarted. *Our* expectation – not *Kent's*. He seems content simply to be present.

Kent's last interaction with Lear is a series of interruptions, Shakespeare closely mimicking the kind of real overlapping one might expect in such a fraught situation:

LEAR
This is a dull sight. Are you not Kent?

KENT
                             The same –
Your servant Kent: Where is your servant Caius?   **+1**

LEAR
He's a good fellow, I can tell you that;
He'll strike, and quickly too. He's dead and rotten.

KENT
No, my good lord; I am the very man –

LEAR
I'll see that straight. (x \ x \ x \ )   **-6**

KENT
That from your first of difference and decay,   **+2**
Have followed your sad steps –

LEAR
                       You are welcome hither. **+2**

KENT
Nor no man else. All's cheerless, dark, and deadly.   **+2**

Analysing the metre in the regular way I've explained, it's still hard to make this flow well, and pace is always a good thing towards the very end of a heavy tragedy. Some have suggested the dialogue really does overlap. I've reset the lines below, and starred the points when the two might be speaking *underneath* each other's lines:

KENT	**LEAR**
	This is a dull sight. Are you not* Kent?
*The same your servant Kent: Where is your servant Caius?	
	He's a good fellow, I can tell you that; He'll strike, and quickly too. He's dead and rotten. *I'll see that straight.
No, my good Lord, I am the very man* that from your first of difference and decay have follow'd your sad steps,* nor no man else...	*You are welcome hither.

🗩 SPEECH LEAR'S FINAL SPEECH

Quite simply, one of the most heartbreaking speeches in the entire canon, as Lear grieves over the body of his beloved daughter Cordelia, all too soon reunited before they're parted again:

LEAR
And my poor **fool** is hanged! No, no, no life!
Why should a dog, a horse, a rat have life
And thou no breath at all? Thou'lt **come** no more;
Never, never, never, never, never.
Pray you undo this button. Thank you sir.
Do you see **this**? Look on her! Look her lips!
Look there! Look there!

fool = dear; meaning Cordelia, but often mistaken to mean the Fool

come = speak

this – Lear dies with the belief he sees Cordelia move her lips, still yet alive

As discussed earlier (see FIVE INTERVAL WHISPERS, p.30), the line of trochaic pentameter of *Never, never…*, turning the rhythm of the poetry back to front as Lear's world – Cordelia – lies dead before him, is wrenching.

Emotionally drained, physically exhausted (after having – amazingly – killed Cordelia's hangman), he asks for someone to undo a button, presumably restricting his breath, indicative of a coming heart attack. Moving from the hugeness of never hearing someone speak again, to the poignant detail of a button, the writing is utterly beautiful and ambitious in its scale.

🗩 SPEECH EDGAR

The final lines of the play, spoken by the heir apparent, a man who has been on a very Hamlet-ian journey of student, madman, warrior-king. The lines were originally given to Albany (see AFTER, pp.97–8), and the final rhyme, which falters a little in most modern English accents, worked better in Shakespeare's time (*young* would have been pronounced *yong*):

EDGAR
The weight of this sad time we must obey,
Speak what we feel, not what we ought to say.
The oldest have borne most; we that are young
Shall never see so much, nor live so long.
[Exeunt with a dead march]

There is something wonderful about this terribly simple advice being given to you by a man who has had to grow up in the most violent way. Edgar, a sort of mild, bookish man, becomes a warrior, then sees this holocaust, and the advice he gives you is, open your heart, speak what you feel…

Sir Richard Eyre

☞ WORDS

• *he **compeers** the best* = equals, matches
• *you so looked **asquint*** = with prejudice
• *If not, I'll ne'er trust **medicine*** = poison; Goneril has poisoned Regan, presumably to ensure her future with Edmund?
• ***maugre** thy strength* = in spite of; pronounced *maw-guh*; Edgar, after his time of poverty, is likely to be weaker and less well-equipped than his battle-ready brother
• *treason's truth bare-gnawn and **canker**-bit* = a canker is something that eats away
• *the wheel is come full circle; **I am here*** = Edmund acknowledges Fortune's part to play, and becomes fully present, perhaps for the first time; see AFTER (p.93)
• *his grief grew **puissant*** = powerful, strong

AFTER

Every night I referred to it as 'climbing on board the juggernaut' or 'climbing Everest', but certainly climbing, and there was a real sense of the verse and the drama pulling you forward with great compulsion and urgency. After each performance I would feel drained and exhausted, though consumed in a very different way from a Pinter play. With Lear there was a physical weariness that was similar to the feebleness one experiences after extreme exercise.

Sir Ian Holm

When I'm asked which is my favourite play in the canon, I pretend to hesitate, but it's been *Lear* for years. I despised it at school, but the more I get to know it, the more I love it.

Most people will say *Hamlet*, and while the *Tragedy of the Prince of Denmark* is filled with some of the most amazing thoughts, the play has plot-holes in it the size of tanks. For me, *King Lear* is a perfect play.

That is, in terms of what constitutes a great play: a strong plot, which is underpinned and interwoven with an equally solid subplot, before the two meet at the end; wonderful characters who speak their minds and hearts in terrific poetry; some uses of the metre which are nothing short of genius; and a fourth quarter which drives towards hope of reconciliation brilliantly and brutally withdrawn from us; and bloody revenge, complete with a huge sword-fight.

It's a great model for a play, and Shakespeare had played around with a similar structure in *Hamlet* already, and was about to do it again with *Macbeth* – although neither has as strong a subplot as *Lear*.

Some say the plot is defective, especially as the story in the original source (that Shakespeare based his play on) ends happily (the Poet Laureate Nahum Tate restored the happy ending, see below). But Shakespeare's version is a tragedy through and through, full of huge ideas about mortality.

It's disorienting, and upsetting. Twice we are denied the resolution we yearn for. The reconciliation of Edgar and Gloucester takes place off-stage, and while we see Kent reveal his true identity to Lear, it's skimmed over. It's as if Shakespeare deliberately slaps us in the face whenever we begin to feel hopeful, reminding us that life can sometimes be relentless, and dark.

Even the ending is deceptively hopeful. The possibility of a fresh, new beginning, the chink of light at the end of the tunnel in Edgar's rise to the throne is a *sliver* of sad hope after one of the most gruelling, heartbreaking, almost relentlessly painful three hours of drama that has graced English theatre. Its beauty and brilliance come from its writer's attempts to plumb the very depths of his, and humanity's, soul.

The name 'King' means 'He who has the last word, the absolute despot.' It is intoxicating to have such power but it can create deep and unknown problems.

Peter Brook, 2013

LEAR, KING

Why does Lear decide to split the map at the beginning? There is no right answer; what's more, it's a question Shakespeare doesn't tackle either. Whatever motivation Lear has in splitting up his country is left to a production to answer for themselves, and the audience to decide from the actor's choices.

Is Lear an idealist, foolish enough to think that he could rule as overall King as three others sub-rule for him? Is he not a particularly good King, and simply makes a foolish decision? Is he grieving from the death of his wife, or so vain and egotistical that he does it only to hear testament of his daughters' love. Are we being shown the inherent problem of thinking that a deity should, or could, also be an emotional human?

Does the decision come from the source of his madness, a developing dementia, the beginning signs of Alzheimer's Disease, as his ageing brain begins to crumble? Degenerative symptoms often present themselves as poor judgement, misguided planning and ineffective problem-solving. It seems to be a less respected idea in Britain, as the part of Lear has been cast younger and younger over the last few years of productions – in a 2010 RSC production he was played by an actor in his 50s.

True, due to the average lifespan of the average man in Shakespeare's time, that might be closer to the age of the actor who originally played the part, but – particularly in the 20th century – it was until recently reserved for the older stalwarts of the stage.

Playing Lear is now the final jewel in the crown of any great (predominantly male) leading Shakespearean actor. Although the parts *could* be played at any age, the general idea is that the jump goes from the Romeo-age characters in your teens or early 20s, to Hamlet in your 30s, Macbeth in your 40s (and Leontes in *The Winter's Tale* around the same time), Prospero in *The Tempest*… and then, finally, your reward is Lear.

You think, 'Hell, not much longer to play Romeo, or Hamlet,' then it's soon: 'I'm going to be too old for Macbeth.' But you know it's all right, Lear's always there.

Sir Ian McKellen, 2013

Shakespeare's focal point is Lear's tragedy, as he stumbles blindly around trying to find truth in his own increasingly erratic actions. When we see a King fall from grace, it's hard not to be reminded of our own mortality, and the mortality of our own parents. Some societies take great care of their elderly, bringing them into family homes to care for them in their infirmity, instead of the easier road, to write them off and divide up the spoils of their life on this planet.

You're being offered Lear because you are too old to play Hamlet... That means that you have a lot of life experience, which you need to bring to this. That feeling of mortality, if not just around the corner, is at least on the horizon.

John Shrapnel, 2012

THE WORLD OF LEAR
Albion

There's a line in this play that has always caught my attention. At the end of 3:2 the Fool talks of a wizard from fabled history:

> **FOOL**
> This prophecy Merlin shall make, for I live before his time.

Halfway through the play, the Fool steps outside of the action and speaks directly to us, placing us in a time *before* our history's greatest legend, of King Arthur, Merlin, the Knights of the Round Table and the Sword in the Stone. Shakespeare allows him to leave the frame, but only to tell us that *he and his fellows* are even further away from *our* frame.

The real King Arthur ruled Britain in the 5th-6th century, but the popular romantic version of his story dates later, to 12th-century France, and it is this more ethereal tale the Fool is marking.

We are, then, stepping into a parallel history where magic may come to exist, a land where Kings can call on the Gods for help, and curse others with sickness The idea is hinted at earlier, in 2:2, when Kent rails at Oswald, and mentions the castle Camelot, and again at the end of 3:4, with Edgar's Childe Rowland reference.

So while the Map (BEFORE, p.22) can be useful in terms of the places mentioned, the play is almost intentionally place-less. The geography of the play is deliberately agoraphobic, and we – not to mention most of the characters – are lost in flat, empty space.

No one in *Lear* knows where they are, or where the Court – the seat of power and focal point of law and order – is located, once the King begins to travel around. The opening courtly scene specifies no city – and certainly not London, where Shakespeare's monarch resided.

There is no bona fide religion to have faith in – though *Lear* is a play saturated in Christianity, even if it's not readily visible on the surface. Edgar's return at the end of the play has a Christ-like feel to it, driven to despair by the Devil-Edmund, before arriving out of the wilderness on the call of the third trumpet.

Gods

Lear calls on the gods when he most needs help – it is his able right as King. The monarch was seen as the Christian God's spokesperson on Earth, but it was the Greek and Roman gods who were once thought to come down and assist mortals.

Gloucester's *Give me some help! O, you Gods* in 4:7, and Lear's *you see me here, you gods* in 2:4 continue to bring an other-worldly feel to the play. The King even calls on the Queen of Witches when he disowns Cordelia in 1:1 – *the mysteries of Hecat and the night* – but unlike *Cymbeline* or *As You Like It*, the gods are silent, and never come to aid these characters.

Nature

One of the most famous scenes in the play is 3:2, where Lear, having left Gloucester's Castle, finds himself without followers and alone in the countryside, with only the Fool at his side. He raves at the growing storm, and it's unclear whether he's encouraging or creating it. Productions have played both ways, and reimagined the manifestation of such a storm in countless ways, from having it actually rain on the stage, to using simple sound effects (see below, p.101). Does Lear, through his monarchic power, begin the storm, or is it a symbol of the turmoil in his mind?

The constant references to Nature, the mother of Earth and all things natural-born, subtly remind us of an invisible feminine presence in a play that lacks any maternal human figure.

THE FEMALE OF THE SPECIES

Shakespeare is somewhat well-known for absent women. He spent a lot of his life in London while his wife was in Stratford-upon-Avon; scholars frequently write about the real-life identity of the Dark Lady character in his Sonnets. His plays are full of missing ladies too.

Leonato's wife in *Much Ado About Nothing*, the brothers Antipholus' mother in *Comedy of Errors* (who does have a cameo towards the end of the play), Shylock's wife and Jessica's mother in *The Merchant of Venice*, Prospero's wife and Miranda's mother in *The Tempest*, Perdita's mother in *The Winter's Tale* (for a while), Innogen's mother in *Cymbeline*, Pericles' wife and Marina's mother in *Pericles*…

Lear's wife is notable by her absence too, aside from a fleeting half-reference by Lear, who, threatening Regan, implores: *divorce me from thy mother's tomb / Sepulchring an adult'ress*. The effects of the dead Queen's life, though, are more than evident – in the daughters she had with Lear, around whom the play's story spins. As Lear's wife gave him no son and therefore no direct heir to the throne, this may have given rise to his breaking up of the country at the beginning of the play.

Another non-human female figure dominates the play though: Fortune.

Fortuna, and her Wheel

The Roman Goddess Fortuna, blind and spinning her Wheel of Fortune. Those at the top of the wheel, enjoying success and happiness, eventually roll to the bottom, to endure misery and suffering. The miserable rise to the top and joy comes to them.

The famous piece of music, *Carmina Burana*, features the lyrics:

The wheel of Fortune turns;
I go down, demeaned;
another is carried to the height;
far too high up
sits the king at the summit –
let him beware ruin!

The idea echoes with Lear's fall, his own image of himself on the 'wheel of fire', and Kent's plea directly to Fortune once he's placed in the stocks: *Fortune ... smile once more, turn thy wheel.*

It's a major theme of a slightly earlier tragedy, as Macbeth, sitting around 9.30pm on the Wheel of Fortune, rises as high as you can go by becoming King, only to immediately begin crashing back down to the bottom.

Edmund's *The wheel is come full circle; I am here* is an acknowledgement of humanity's inability to control events, that something other might be in control; that in one's rise another falls. His final *I am here* brings him to the present moment in a way he has, in all his aspiring dreamings of a seemingly unobtainable future, hitherto not experienced.

MADNESS, SEEING, AND BLINDNESS

The term *fall from grace* was never truer. In a land devoid of religion, with its inhabitants ruled by the Wheel of Fortune, Planetary Gods and curses, a King (the mouthpiece through which God would speak in Shakespeare's time) through his own foolishness is stripped of power and goes mad.

Blind to the truth of his daughters' love, and his country's need for a strong ruler, Lear doesn't see how far he's let things slip until he lies in squalor with the beggar Poor Tom-a-Bedlam. Even then, the real truth evades him, as he doesn't recognise Edgar behind the beggarly disguise. Lear's fall from grace reaches its nadir when the Wheel of Fortune has turned 180 degrees from fortune to ill-fortune.

Only then can he begin to regain his wits, climb back towards grace, his throne, and a more fortunate time. The same goes for Gloucester, who doesn't see the truth of Edmund's deception and Edgar's loyalty until he's been blinded and fallen to ill-fortune.

It's interesting that in his choice of disguise, Edgar chooses as his model a servant who has gone mad and believes he's being chased by the devil. When he is surprised in his hidey-hole hovel by the King, his Fool, and later, his father, he must be improvising wildly.

Using a well-known stereotype, the beggarman Tom o'Bedlam (an inmate of the old London insane asylum Bethlehem Hospital), he begins to take on the role. The character he builds is an extraordinary feat of imagination. 'Tom' describes himself as

> *false of heart, light of ear, bloody of hand; hog in sloth, fox in stealth, wolf in greediness, dog in madness, lion in prey*

which gives great inspiration to the actor for the animal-like physicality Tom might have.

He repeatedly says the words *Tom's a-cold* – essentially telling the others, or muttering to himself, that he's cold – as he would be, dressed only in a blanket at night, with no protection from the storm.

Sometimes he dives off into a distant world, where he sees the devil biting his back; at others he seems remarkably lucid. There's a lovely character note when Lear leaves at the end of 3:7 and Edgar immediately releases his Poor Tom character. It is all an act, and one in which he never loses himself entirely.

THE CHILDREN OF MEN

Every single character in the play is extraordinarily full and three-dimensional. There have been productions which have Goneril, Regan, Cornwall and Edmund as simply utterly evil, making them almost pantomimic, devoid of any goodness – but they're far more complex than that.

Lear's eldest daughters are often thought of as lying, manipulative, evil witches because of the way they respond to Lear's request, and their later treatment of him. Cordelia is right when she says she can't *heave her heart into a tongue*, and that she doesn't want to marry someone if she *loves her father all*. But, playing the political game that Lear has asked them to play, their only real choice is to give him what he wants, and do it to the best of their ability.

Similar to the manipulative Edmund, villains never think themselves evil – Goneril and Regan believe they're in the right. Few characters – if any – in Shakespeare are purely malevolent, and if they seem so, like Richard III or Aaron the Moor (in *Titus Andronicus*), they're equally given a quality which makes us admire them in some way – Richard's sense of humour and Aaron's love for his child.

So while Regan incites Cornwall to (and in some productions, participates in) the blinding of Gloucester and his psychopathically horrendous torture, she still seems to dearly love her husband, and once he's died her move towards Edmund is as shrewd a political move as Gertrude's is to Claudius in *Hamlet*.

Goneril is no less complex. She's right in her complaint in 1:4; it *is* unreasonable to have two different figures of authority – two monarchs, essentially – in one household, however big that house may be, and despite the fact that her guest is her King and father.

Whether or not she is being entirely truthful when she describes Lear's knights as being unruly is open to question – are the knights played in that scene as Arthurian Knights of the Round Table, wearing gleaming silver, or are they drunken rogues?

Her husband Albany seems at first mild-mannered, and then rebels against the direction she takes as her treatment of Lear worsens. Amusingly, King James' two sons were the Dukes of Albany and Cornwall, and saw the play at Court on Boxing Day in 1606 (the inherent warning on British unity, as Lear's Britain falls apart, would not have gone unnoticed). Equally desirous for power, Goneril ends up poisoning her sister and taking her own life; she spirals into a pseudo-Lady Macbeth.

But do the sisters plot from the start to ruin Lear, or it an idea that blossoms? Their father has just made an enemy with France, the country nearest to the one they now jointly rule. They'd need to be especially close – in both familial and political relationships – in order to rule effectively and stay strong in case of war. It's only later that the desire for individual power tears them apart.

Edmund, Bastard

The sisters' love for each other seems strong, but is quickly splintered in their desire to gain Edmund. Once they turn against each other, and if Edgar's final acceptance of a single crown is anything to go by, perhaps the bastard son of Gloucester is seen by both Queens as the way back to sole leadership of the realm. A younger and inexperienced but powerful leader that they could reward and then manipulate….

Like Macbeth, having gained a certain amount of ground, Edmund is not only greedy for more, he wants to ensure the stability of his condition. Any fallout from tricking Gloucester into making him the rightful heir is avoided by betraying him to Cornwall. To marry a Queen would be a huge social elevation for him, and a vast improvement on merely becoming heir to Gloucester's lands and title.

Edmund is right too, of course. It *is* unfair that simply because his father had sex with a woman he wasn't married to, *he's* considered a lesser person by society, suffering at the hands of sociological segregation. He does what he can to stop his life being filled with poverty and misery, and gain some power and control. Like the sisters, like Macbeth, he quickly spirals out of control and becomes villainous.

Edmund is an interesting protagonist because we see him wrestle with the idea of doing evil before he submits to it. Playing him uniformly as a moustache-twirling wrong-doer is less dramatically interesting than watching someone who believes he's doing what needs to be done to survive, however evil that action may be. It's what transforms a two-dimensional character into a real human being.

SIDE-NOTE
Shakespeare's younger brother came to London, worked as an actor, died two years after *King Lear* was written, and was buried in Southwark Cathedral, a few minutes' walk from the Globe. Father to an illegitimate son named Edward and 16 years Shakespeare's junior, he was christened Edmund. Whether the character of Edmund was written as a compliment – or an insult – to him has been a source of great debate and we'll never know, but the parallels fascinate biographers.

Get a Cordelia you can carry, and watch your Fool.
Sir Donald Wolfit (1902–68)

A FOOL, AN ALLOWED FOOL...
The Fool has been cast as a young boy-man, and has often been doubled with Cordelia – either as an easy piece of double-casting as they never appear in a scene together, or to play with the idea that Cordelia disguises herself as the Fool in order to stay close to her Father. Either way, the Fool's pining since Cordelia's banishment tells of a close bond between them – he would have been Grandfather, bed-time story-teller, party-clown and comforter to her – or perhaps sorrow entirely due to his master's own foolishness. He's equally often been played by an older man, of a similar age to Lear, implying a jester who has been with Lear all his life.

The Fool disappears halfway through the play and isn't referred to again. Some describe this as a mistake on Shakespeare's part; others interpret it as very fitting – that Lear is past the point of being able to appreciate the philosophy and lessons the Fool has to offer, choosing instead to listen to the mad ramblings of Poor Tom.

Fools in Shakespeare's later plays like *Twelfth Night* had a counsellor role. They were the wisdom behind the smile. Fools or Jesters originally wore colourful motley (patchwork) clothes and bells as part of their entertaining distraction. Shakespeare used the colours and sounds as a mask, behind which they could hide and be the teller of any truth, an 'allowed' fool, who could do no wrong. Perhaps, in a modern production, their mask could be a beautiful body?

Yet they're intended to be a-sexual – in that their role is not to be sexual, but to be comedic and wise, usually at the same time. And though there is rarely a fitting response to their sayings, it is not out of another's ignorance – their wisdom requires no answer.

The child-like name the Fool uses – *Nuncle* – makes him, in essence, a living child, a constant reminder of the mistake Lear made with his children, who plays out in words the truth Lear's stubbornness cannot keep at bay.

TATE'S LEAR

Once the theatres were reopened in 1660 (following the end of the Puritanical regime, which forbad plays and public entertainment), Restoration comedies by Wycherley, Congreve and his contemporaries came to the theatres. Farcical, slapstick, bawdy romps were what brought people in; after the cultural desert of the last decade and a half, no one wanted heavy, sad, serious plays, though *Hamlet* and *Othello* (not exactly light pieces) were still popular.

Not wanting to lose some of the greatest plays by Shakespeare, writers began to reimagine the tragedies – Romeo and Juliet survive! – and one of the more notorious is the Poet Laureate Nahum Tate's *The History of King Lear* (1681).

Most of Shakespeare's plays are retellings of famous stories – his was not the only *Henry V* play doing the rounds of the theatres – and there are plenty of recent adaptations of Shakespeare's plays. While some are considered to be good reworkings – Edward Bond's *Lear* is an excellent example (see below, p.104) – Tate's 1681 reworking tears Shakespeare's work apart.

Returning to the happy ending of the source story, Cordelia and Edgar fall in love with each other; she survives, and everyone spends a lot of time talking about how mad Lear is. Any subtlety found in Shakespeare's version is sadly missing, but until the mid-19th century Tate's was the most popular *Lear* around.

QUARTO vs FOLIO versions

King Lear comes in two sizes – the Quarto of 1608, and the Folio of 1623. Quite literally two sizes, as in Shakespeare's time a *quarto* copy meant a book made up with pieces of paper folded twice; a *folio* was made up from paper folded once, so was about twice the size of a quarto. Plays were rarely published in folio – due to their size they were more expensive, and more portentously regarded, so were usually reserved for the 'high art' of poetry and science.

In terms of text, there's quite a difference between the 1608 Quarto, published while Shakespeare was still writing, and the 1623 Folio, published seven years after his death. Often a production will make an amalgamation of the two texts, using the Folio as the starting point, and taking the best extra bits from the Quarto.

There are around 285 lines in the Quarto not found in the Folio, and 115 in the Folio not found in the Quarto. Some lines – and even some speeches – are reattributed to other characters. An entire scene, Act 4:3 (between Kent and the Gentlemen, discussing Cordelia and Lear) is found in the Quarto version, but not in the Folio. Indeed, it is often cut in productions.

It's been argued that the Folio version is Shakespeare's own reworking – a second, post-performance draft – and was adapted not just to make the play generally tighter, but to weaken the characters of Albany and Kent and make Edgar stronger, better setting him up as the future King.

One of the more interesting differences between the two is in the final moments of *Lear*:

Quarto text:

LEAR
And my poor fool is hanged. No, no life?
Why should a dog, a horse, a rat have life,
And thou no breath at all? O, thou wilt come no more,
Never, never, never.
Pray you, undo this button. Thank you, sir.
O, O, O, O.

EDGAR
He faints. My lord, my lord!

And Lear dies a few lines later. The Folio text finishes the *Never, never…* line, which as we've seen (p.84) is quite staggeringly beautiful:

LEAR
And my poor fool is hanged. No, no, no life?
Why should a dog, a horse, a rat have life,
And thou no breath at all? Thou'lt come no more,
Never, never, never, never, never.
Pray you, undo this button. Thank you, sir.
Do you see this? Look on her! Look, her lips.
Look there, look there. [He dies]

EDGAR
He faints. My lord, my lord!

The Folio also adds two extra lines, as Lear believes in his dying moments that Cordelia is still alive, that her lips are moving, and so perhaps – even in delusion – dies a little happier than before.

MORE THAN TEN...

As I've indicated earlier in this book, there's some extended metrical analysis that can be done to unpack the parts. A lot of people disagree with the process, and it puts an incredible amount of faith both in the writer and those printing his works, neither of who were necessarily sober when creating.

However, it's a process that has helped me and others in the rehearsal room, so I'd suggest it's worth looking at some of the speeches in the DURING section to see if anything interesting comes up.

If Shakespeare had wanted a line of metre to be ten syllables long, he was skilled enough to make it so. If it's more than ten, there might be something to note about what the character is saying.

When there are more than ten syllables in a line of poetry, I've put a **+1** or **+2** next to the line:

EDGAR

I will preserve myself; and am bethought
To take the basest and most poorest shape   +1
That e'er **penury**, in contempt of man,
Brought <u>near to beast.</u>

Here, the thought Edgar is trying to convey tries to flow over the metrical line, but is restrained by it. A nobleman contemplates disguising himself as a beggar, and the metre wrinkles slightly; a clue to the actor about Edgar's feelings at this point – it's likely the image of poverty makes him uncomfortable – and ultimately a piece of his character jigsaw puzzle.

A quick look at the numbers to the right-hand side of the speeches can give an emotional flow-chart for the character:

- When there's a **+2** or a **-4**, *something* is happening or being said that resonates more strongly with the character, indicating a less calm state of mind
- When there isn't a number, then there's a regular number of syllables in the line of metre, and the character's more in control of what they're saying

Frankly, Lear is an easy part, one of the easiest in Shakespeare, apart from Coriolanus. We can all play it. It is simply bang straightforward. Not like Romeo for instance, where you spend the whole evening searching for sympathy. But then anyone who lets an erection rule his life doesn't deserve sympathy, does he?
Sir Laurence Olivier (1907–89)

TAKING YOUR EXPERIENCE FURTHER...

Everyone has their own opinion on how a Shakespeare play should be performed or produced. All the performance options and questions Shakespeare has left us, and how they have been met – or ignored – will directly affect your response to the play. Here are the main parameters.

THE USE OF THE SPACE

Partly dependent on the type of space the play was performed in (a theatre, a wood, a warehouse, or an old shopping mall...)

– Whether the audience was seated all around the stage, along two sides, or end-on to the performance, and whether the configuration intentionally created sight-line issues (to obscure a piece of stage business)
– Whether parts of the set came from above or beneath the stage, or were moved on or off from the sides
– Whether the actors engaged with the audience, interacted with them or moved through them – in other words, whether the playing space and the auditorium were fused together, or kept distinct and separate

THE DESIGN

Different from how the space is used by the actors, the design of the show can set the play in a particular time or period, perhaps to try to reflect a particular issue. It could be 16th-century England, a modern-day council estate, the Second World War or a non-place harder to distinguish from the set but perhaps indicated by costume from a particular period – formal military or army clothes, Victorian clothes, or office suits.

– A non-space might rely on lighting effects to aid the location shift from the heath to the various castles
– Some productions are prop-heavy, using lots of objects to help tell the story; some only use a coxcomb and a single feather
– Considering the number of people who are killed, there could be a lot of stage-blood, or something else used to signify 'blood'

THE STRUCTURE

This is an oft-produced play, and sometimes extraordinary efforts are made to try to do something new with it. Those efforts are usually made in the setting, which combination of Folio and Quarto is used, and how many lines have been cut, as it's a difficult play to remove entire scenes from.

Some things to consider in terms of the overall aesthetic of the production.

– Whether there was an interval, and if it felt well-placed – could it have come earlier?

- Whether any of the actors played more than one part: in smaller-scale productions, actors often double-up the parts they play (Burgundy and France with Lear's Knights); sometimes the doubling can have interesting effects (the Fool with Cordelia)
- Whether many (or any) lines of text, or the order of the scenes were changed to tell the story in a different way. An account of which edition of the play they used is sometimes mentioned in the production's programme
- If something was cut, it could have been omitted to help make the production setting work better, or simply to make the running time shorter. The full text of *Lear* runs to nearly four hours, so something is usually snipped out

THE FOOL

As I discussed earlier, the room for interpretation in this part is enormous.

- The Fool has been getting older over the last twenty years of productions. Casting swings between a younger Fool and an older man, similar in years to Lear, giving the impression of someone who has been a fool to him since birth
- Sometimes the actor has pushed for a funnier rather than a philosophical Fool. In an RSC production in 1982 a young Sir Antony Sher played him as a capering, juggling, circus-like European clown. In Sir Ian Holm's powerful *King Lear* at the National Theatre in 1997, David Burke's Fool was as old as Lear, but much wiser and sadder.

THE STORM

Productions have presented the storm in a number of ways:

- In 1999 the Japanese director Ninagawa (see Websites, below) dropped huge rocks from the top of the theatre down onto the stage, to simulate the terrible storm
- Productions have built in a rain-system, to soak the stage and the actors
- Others have used lighting and sound effects for thunder, while others still have only a bare stage and the actors' voices, as they mime the strong winds and heavy rains

THE ENDING

How you end a dark, tragic drama is a difficult question, and every production will be different.

- The standard 20th-century close is a slow fade out of the lights to black, often with solemn drums
- The more traditional ending that Shakespeare's audience would have expected was celebratory, with music and a dance.
- But if you're reading the play – how would you end it?

LIKE OR UNLIKE

If you were experiencing the play for the first time:

- Did you think it was going to be difficult to understand? And was it?
- Did the production you see change the ideas you had about the play, whether they were good or bad?
- And... would you go and see it again?

WHERE TO SPRING NEXT...?

You've experienced one of Shakespeare's greatest tragedies, so what now?

If you've been reading the play
- buy a different edition of the play, and read a different editor's introduction
- go to see a staged production
- watch a film version

If you've been to see a production, do you want to
- watch another production of the same play and see how it differs?
- read – or re-read – the text, to see which bits were left out? and bring together your memories of the performance with the script in front of you: perhaps some lines or scenes were cut, considered too difficult to understand, or they didn't fit with the director's vision of the play; can you see why the actors, director, and designers made the decisions they made?

Or dive straight into another Shakespeare play
- another tragedy, perhaps *Macbeth* (a blood-soaked tragedy of regicide, madness, ghosts and witches) or *Othello* (an absolute look at love, passion and jealousy)
- head to *Henry V*, Shakespeare's historical account of the Boy Who Would Be King as he rises to lead his country against France, or *Richard II*, one of his most poetically beautiful plays, with the tragic fall of the King Who Would Be Boy
- the mistaken identity almost-farce of *The Comedy of Errors*, or the lovers, fairies and forestry sexual shenanigans of *A Midsummer Night's Dream*, both with a dark heart hidden at their cores.

You have a selection of thirty-nine plays in all, offering an exploration of the human heart and mind in ways that are quite starkly different from each other, whether you're reading them, watching them in a theatre or on screen, yet all linked by one writer, his imagination, and his rather deft ability with the quill.

I've listed some books, films, theatres and companies below. Anything mentioned will point you in different directions in the recent Shakespeare-related world.

It all depends where you'd like to spring next.

SPRINGBOARDS

Below, some carefully chosen, *Lear*-related books, films and websites to consider.

PRINT

King Lear (Arden Shakespeare, 1997)
Edited by the American literary scholar and author R. A. Foakes, his introduction focuses on the staging of the play over the years, and the various sources that inspired Shakespeare's version. The notes (see the *Guide to Other Texts*, below) are comprehensive, and have a strong literary-critical bent.

The Fool (Anchor Books, 1961)
If the idea of the Fool, or court jester, intrigues you, then Enid Welsford's detailed social and literary history of this sadly now extinct-in-real-life character is fascinating.

Lear (Methuen, 1983)
The British playwright Edward Bond's 1971 epic, violent and bloody modern rewrite of Shakespeare's *King Lear*. The language, while beautiful, is sparse; the play is bleak, but it can serve as a good bridge back to Shakespeare.

A Shakespeare Miscellany (Penguin, 2005)
David and Ben Crystal's coffee-table quiz-book of facts about Shakespeare's life, language and plays, together with descriptions of Elizabethan life and theatre, quotes from well-known Shakespeare actors, and anecdotes of modern film and theatre productions of the plays.

The RSC Shakespeare: The Complete Works (Palgrave Macmillan, 2008)
A recent edition of Shakespeare's works closely based on the First Folio. Edited by the literary scholars Jonathan Bate and Eric Rasmussen, with notes suggesting staging possibilities of each scene.

The Oxford Companion to Shakespeare (OUP, 2005)
Stanley Wells and Michael Dobson's straightforward and well laid-out play-by-play companion to Shakespeare's works, life and times.

Contested Will (James Shapiro, Faber, 2010)
A detective-like analysis of the conspiracy theories surrounding the authorship of the plays and poems, by the American scholar James Shapiro, accounting the various (slightly mad) historical figures' fascination with the author responsible for the plays written under the name of Shakespeare.

GUIDE TO OTHER TEXTS OF THE PLAY

If you decide to move on to an edited text of the play, it will be filled with notes, either below the text, to the side, or at the back of the book. Years of study and editing have crammed these plays with commentary, asides and questions.

Notes

They can be daunting to look at if you're not used to them. Many will tell you what a word means, or that there's an allusion to the Bible, but depending on when it was written, there may not be a reason given as to why the character might have chosen that particular word, or what it could mean to them or the audience that a biblical reference was made.

Names like Theobald or Malone may appear from time to time, referring to earlier editors of the plays. The interpretations and textual emendations they suggested to solve problems in the text are often referenced.

F vs Q

Some will mention words or spellings being F or Q1, Q2, etc. – which means the spellings have been taken by the editor from the Folio, the First Quarto printing, the Second Quarto printing, etc.

Names and stage directions

Some will supplement the sparse Folio stage directions with full locations and descriptions of what the characters may be doing, which are either implied in the text or based on the editor's interpretation.

FILM

Game of Thrones (2011–)

Adapted from George R. R. Martin's series of fantasy novels, this TV series captures an age-old world, filled with foolish Kings, a duplicitous Queen, loyal (and treacherous) subjects, chess-like political aligning and back-stabbing duplicity, as people vie for the crown. Echoes of Kent, Regan, Oswald abound, and the world of *King Lear* will make a little more sense for watching it.

King Lear (1983)

Sir Laurence Olivier, the master Shakespearean of the 20th century, gives his Lear, with John Hurt as his Fool. Dated, but a piece of craftsmanship by an actor who spent his career bringing Shakespeare to life.

King Lear (1997)

The BBC film of the National Theatre's stage version, which was artistic director Sir Richard Eyre's farewell to the building, and Sir Ian Holm's return to the stage after twenty years. Staggering.

King Lear (1971)

Nearly ten years after their RSC production, two theatrical masters of the 20th century come together in director Peter Brook and Shakespearean legend Sir Paul Scofield. The minimalist style, lack of music, and quiet, boiling power from Scofield makes for a thrilling, eerie experience.

Korol Lir (1971)
Nothing less than epic, Grigori Korinstev's opening court scene strikes a scale bigger than a theatre production could easily hit, and the stylised storm scene is sublime. But it is in Russian, so be warned.

Life Goes on (2009)
Sangeeta Datta's adaptation of Lear, retold via a Hindu family living in London; it's a delicate and beautifully sentimental modern adaptation.

Ran (1985)
Akira Kurosawa's epic adaptation of Shakespeare's tragedy in a Japanese setting, and two masters of their craft meet with a third, as the acclaimed Japanese actor Tatsuya Nakadai takes the Lear character equivalent.

WEB
Pointing towards Shakespeare Theatre Companies or excellent online media resources

The British Library – www.bl.uk
List, view scans, and compare 107 different copies of the 21 plays printed in Quarto before the theatre closures of 1642.

Bell Shakespeare Company – www.bellshakespeare.com.au
A leading Australian Shakespeare company, based out of Sydney, with a terrific education programme.

The Folger Library – www.folger.edu
The largest collection of Shakespeare material in the world, located in Washington DC.

The National School of Drama Theatre Festival Delhi – www.nsdtheatrefest.com
Held over two weeks every January in Delhi, often featuring over half a dozen productions or (usually fairly radical) adaptations of Shakespeare plays.

Play Shakespeare – www.playshakespeare.com
An excellent free to use collection of Shakespeare's works, reviews of productions and books, together with a broad online community, allowing festivals and companies across the world to network. Builders of the iPhone Shakespeare App.

The Royal Shakespeare Company – www.rsc.org.uk
Three newly refurbished theatres with an ensemble company playing year-round

in Shakespeare's home town. The website has a great deal of audio and visual interviews and clips of productions.

The Shakespeare Institute – http://www.birmingham.ac.uk/Shakespeare
The internationally renowned research institution, established to 'push the boundaries of knowledge about Shakespeare studies and Renaissance drama'.

Shakespeare's Globe – www.shakespearesglobe.org
The reconstructed Shakespeare's Globe Theatre, London, with details both of their main summer theatre season and their extraordinary winter education season.

Shakespeare's Globe, Neuss – www.shakespeare-festival.de/en
A replica of Shakespeare's Globe in Neuss, Germany, with a fine festival of plays and a regular receiver of visiting Shakespeare companies.

Shakespeare's Words – www.shakespeareswords.com
The website based on the dictionary, free to use: linguistically explore Shakespeare's works like never before. The Glossary in this book is adapted from this database.

Stratford Shakespeare Festival – www.stratfordfestival.ca
Based out of Stratford, Canada, a highly renowned theatre company with a wide-ranging season respected throughout North America.

Yukio Ninagawa – www.ninagawastudio.net
His company – together with British producers Thelma Holt and the RSC – have been bringing Ninagawa's especial brand of Shakespeare production to the UK since the 1990s. Often thematically expansive, and regularly featuring highly regarded Noh and Kabuki actors.

A SHORT SPRINGBOARD INTO...
THE TAMING OF THE SHREW

A tale of love found, of women, of loss, and now one of the more contentious parts of the canon...

··

☞ THE INDUCTION

One of Shakespeare's first plays, *Shrew* begins with an Induction – essentially, a preamble, telling the story of a drunk, Christopher Sly, who is duped into thinking he is a rich lord. The people tricking him begin to tell him a story, and we enter into the world of the play.

There is no end-scene resolving the Christopher Sly story. In some respects, the theatrical device is redundant by the end of the play, and doesn't need finishing, though in other respects not completing the bookend means the audience leaves the theatre still within the world of *Shrew*. Whether the young playwright Shakespeare was intending to use the device in such a bold way or simply forgot to write a Sly-ending is open to endless debate.

··

☞ CHARACTERS   Kate and Petruchio

Petruchio, at the prospect of a large dowry, agrees to marry the shrewish Kate (*shrew* meant a bad-tempered woman), and over the course of the play drags her around the country, starves her and stops her from sleeping, and is generally unkind towards her.

At some point, she stops fighting, and appears to fall in love with him. Or does she fall in love with him at first sight, and they play a dangerous, flirtatious game with each other? Or is she simply 'beaten' into submission? One of the highlights of watching a production is seeing when the actress playing Kate chooses to show us her feelings towards Petruchio have changed, and his for her. To tame the Shrew, you must first love the Shrew.

··

☞ SIDE-NOTE   Feminism

How do you do this play? In our 21st-century, politically correct world, Petruchio's treatment of Kate teeters on criminal abuse. Some have considered it an anti-feminist work, but that has always made less sense to me, considering Shakespeare's other strong female leads, and that *Shrew* was written in a time when his monarch was herself a fearsomely strong woman.

An exploration of love, of a woman's place in society, and man's sense of right as absolute authority, the play has struggled in recent years to be seen clearly without the benefit of Elizabethan eyes. Is the play now, in our time, pro-women, anti-women, or something else?

☞ SPEECH   Kate's final speech

Kate's final, long speech, when she's called to demonstrate the loyalty and faith a wife must have for her husband, is an incredibly hard sell after all she's been through with Petruchio. She ends the speech laying her hand on the floor, asking him to step on her. She seems to mean every word, making her journey from shrew to obedient wife especially tricky to play well. It all hangs on how her relationship with Petruchio has been built up to that point...

☞ CHARACTER   Bianca

Dominated by her father, Kate's shrewishness isn't helped by her prettier, younger sister, who, as Elizabethan society dictated, couldn't marry until her elder sister is packaged off. The wooing of Bianca takes the subplot of the play, as three suitors go to extreme lengths to gain her hand. Supposedly, Bianca is the prom-queen jewel in her father's crown, but as we later see, there's more to Kate than meets the eye, and less character to her sister. Who, after all, ends up the happiest?

GLOSSARY

abated reduced
abatement lessening
abhorred disgusting
abjure swear to abandon
able strengthen [*I'll ~ 'em*]
abroad[1] in the outside world [*news ~*]
abroad[2] away from home [*stir ~*]
abuse deceive [*do not ~ me*]
abused[1] deceived [*~ father, ear ~*]
abused[2] wronged [*mightily ~; was ~; ~ nature*]
abuses you dishonours you
accommodate equip
action-taking taking legal action
addition[1] attributes *or* qualities [*thy ~; such ~; your ~*]
addition[2] external honour [*all th' ~ to a king*]
addition[3] extra assistance [*what ~ I can*]
address speak formally
admirable marvellous
admiration astonishment
ado fuss
advancement preferment
advise warn [*~ the Duke; ~d by aught*]
advise yourself think carefully
affect put on
affected inclined *or* inclined to
afoot[1] in existence [*keep base life ~*]
afoot[2] on the march [*they are ~*]
afore before
ague-proof resistant to sickness
a-height on high
aidant helpful
airs vapours

alarumed stirred to action
allay subside
all-licensed allowed to do anything
allow encourage [*~ obedience*]
allowance permission
allows itself gives itself over
amazed dumbfounded
anatomize dissect
anchoring riding at anchor
ancient[1] former [*for ~ love*]
ancient[2] most experienced [*the ~ of war*]
ancient[3] elderly [*~ ruffian; ~ knave*]
anon soon
answer[1] armed response [*tie him to an ~*]
answer[2] face up to [*~ with thy uncovered body*]
answer[3] be accountable [*~ my life; I'll ~*]
apace quickly
apish ape-like in copying
apothecary medicinal druggist
appertains relates
apprehend seize
apprehension arrest
approve prove *or* confirm
apt ready
arbitrament settlement
arch chief [*~ and patron*]
argument subject
arguments topics
aroynt, aroint be gone
arraign put on trial
arrant absolute
array attire

art skill *or* knowledge

aspect [in astrology] influential phase

asquint in a distorted way

assurance certainty

assured certain

astronomical interpreting the heavens

attaint condemnation

attasked blamed

attempting attacking

attend[1] await [*~ my taking; ~ dispatch; ~ the leisure*]

attend[2] wait on [*~ the lords; ~ him; ~ you*]

attendance diligent service

attended with accompanied by

atwain into two parts

aught anything

auricular audible

authorities powers

avaunt go away

avert redirect

avouch declare

awhile a short time

a-work at work

aye always

bags money-bags

ballow cudgel

balmed soothed

bandy exchange

bans curses

barber-monger frequenter of the barber-shop

bare-gnawn worn away to nothing

bark, barque ship

base[1] low-born [*wherefore ~; ~ ...knave; ~ football player*]

base[2] wretched [*~ life*]

baseness social inferiority

basest[1] lowest-born [*~ ...wretches*]

basest[2] most wretched [*~ beggars; ~ ...shape*]

bastardizing being conceived as a bastard

bat, baton cudgel

battles armies

bawd pimps

beadle parish constable

bearing carrying of hardships [*~ fellowship*]

beastly beast-like [*~ knave*]

become befit *or* honour [*~ a sword; ~s the house; so ~ it*]

bedlam lunatic

Bedlam from Bethlehem Hospital for the insane

before ahead

beget[1] produce [*~ opinion*]

beget[2] conceive [*~ such different issues*]

begot fathered

beguile[1] deceive [*~ the tyrant's rage; cozened and ~d*]

beguile[2] charm [*~d you*]

beholding sight

belike probably

belly-pinched starving

bemadding making mad

be-met encountered

be-monster make monstrous

bend turn

bending overhanging [*~ head*]

benediction blessing

benison blessing

bereaved deprived [*~ sense*]

besort befit

bespoke spoken for

bestirred aroused

bestow[1] lodge [*well ~ed; ~ you*]

bestow[2] give [*~ your needful counsel; fee ~*]

bethink yourself call to your mind

bethought decided

beweep weep over

bewray[1] make known [*thyself ~*]

bewray[2] betray [*~ his practice*]

bias inclination

bide endure

biding place to stay

bills halberds

blame, to to be blamed

blank target centre

block fashion

blood[1] kinship [*property of ~*; *my ~*]

blood[2] nobility [*gentleman of ~*; *in ~*]

blood[3] feelings [*obey my ~*]

blown swollen

bobtail with a docked tail

bold presumptuous [*deboshed and ~*]

bolds makes bold

bond duty [*my ~*]

bondage constraint

boon petition

boot advantage [*with ~*]

boot, to as well

bootless useless

bo-peep peep-bo *or* peek-a-boo

bordered confined

bosom, of her in her confidence

bosomed intimate

bound[1] pledged [*my services are ~*]

bound[2] ready [*~ to take*]

bounds regions

bound to the like required to do the same

bourn boundary [*of England*]

brach or him female or male hound

brave fine [*~ night*]

bravely in fine clothes

brazed hardened

brazen-faced shameless

breath utterance [*makes ~ poor*]

bred brought up

breeding upbringing

brief quick [*be ~ in it*]

briefness speedy action

bring away fetch

broils quarrels

broken left-over [*~ meats*]

brother equal [*not as a ~*; *call itself your ~*]

brow, brows forehead

buoyed up surged

burdocks type of weedy plant

buttered spread butter on

buzz rumour

byle boil

cadent falling

'cagion dialect form of 'occasion' [= reason]

caitiff miserable wretch

canker-bit worm-eaten

capable able to inherit

carbonado slash [as in grilling meat]

carbuncle tumour

carry endure [*~ th'affliction*]

carry it carry it out

case[1] state [*heavy ~*]

case[2] covering [*without a ~*; *~ of eyes*]

casement window

casualties uncertainties

cat civet cat [source of perfumes]

catastrophe denouement

cause court case [*what was thy ~*]

censure[1] blame [*scape ~*]

censure[2] pass judgement on [*~ them*]

censured condemned

cessez [in hunting] off you go

chafes rages

challenged demanded [*~ pity*]

champaigns expanses of open countryside

chance[1] event [*it is a ~*]

chance[2] fortune [*my ~*; *the ~ of anger*]

chance, how how does it happen

character handwriting

charge¹ expense [*at my ~; ~ and danger*]

charge² responsibility [*~ of a star*]

charged commanded

charms magic spells

che dialect form of 'I'

check reprimand

check at turn aside from

chide scold

chiding scolding

child-changed changed by children *or* changed into a child

childed was dealt with by children

'chill dialect form of 'I will'

choice, of specially chosen [*men ~*]

choler anger

choleric inclined to anger

choughs jackdaws

'chould dialect form of 'I should'

civet type of musky perfume

clamor, clamour protest

clap, at a at one stroke

clearest purest

clipped cut short

close concealed [*~ pent-up guilts*]

closet¹ private chamber [*casement of my ~*]

closet² cabinet [*letter in my ~*]

clothier's yard 36"-measure of cloth

clotpoll blockhead

clout bull [in archery]

cock dinghy

cockney squeamish woman

cocks weathercocks

codpiece pouch worn by a man at the front of breeches; *also*, what it contains

cohorts military divisions

coining making coins

colour type [*selfsame ~*]

colours banners

comfortable encouraging

comforting helping

commend¹ present [*~ itself; ~ ... letters*]

commend² entrust [*~ a dear thing*]

commission authority

commit fornicate [*~ not*]

commodities assets

compact¹ allied [*~ and flattering*]

compact² made up [*well ~*]

compact³ consolidate [*~ it more*]

compeers equals

compliment ceremony

composition making up

compounded joined together

conceit imagination

conceive understand

conception thinking [*mine own ~*]

concluded ended

condition nature *or* circumstances

conduct guidance [*quick ~*]

conductor leader

confine domain

confined¹ bounded [*~ deep*]

confined² restricted [*~ to exhibition*]

confusion destruction

conjunct conjoined

consort company

conspirant conspirator

constant resolved

consumption destruction

contemned despised

contemns despises

contending fighting

content¹ contented [*be ~*]

content² happiness [*make ~*]

content³ satisfy [*~ your lord*]

content⁴ calm down [*pray you, ~*]

contented calm

contentious hostile

continent self-controlled

continents containers

control restrain

convenience opportunity
convenient suitable
converse keep company
convey conduct [*~ the business*]
cope face
corky withered
coronet[1] garland [*~ of flowers*]
coronet[2] small crown [*bearing a ~*; *this ~*]
costard head [like an apple]
couch find shelter
countenance[1] expression [*word nor ~*; *in your ~*]
countenance[2] appearance [*~ likes me not*]
countenance[3] position [*~ for the battle*]
course[1] course of action
course[2] habit [*monthly ~*]
course[3] chase [*~ his own shadow*]
courtesan prostitute
court holy-water courtly flattery
cowish cowardly
coxcomb fool's cap *or* head
cozened cheated
cozener cheat
crab crab-apple
crave beg
craves needs
crazed shattered
creature human [*~ runs from the cur*]
credit trust
crewel made of a thin worsted yarn
crime offence
croak growl
cross forked [*~ lightning*]
crosses trials
crow-keeper scarecrow
crown[1] head [*bald ~*]
crown[2] highest point [*~ o'the cliff*]
crowns rounded halves [*~ of the egg*]
cruels forms of cruelty

cry[1] beg [*~ you mercy*; *~ ... grace*]
cry[2] proclaim [*the herald ~*]
cub-drawn ravenous
cuckoo-flower flower growing at the time of year when cuckoos call
cullionly rascally
curiosity scrupulousness
curious finely made
curst angry
cushings cushions
custom habit
cut off take away [*~ my train*]
cutpurses thieves

dally delay
darker more secret
darkling in the dark, in darkness
darnel weeds
dart hurl like an arrow
daub smear
dawning daybreak
deadly death-like
deal[1] amount [*a ~ of man*]
deal[2] speak [*to ~ plainly*]
deal[3] grant [*heavens ~*]
dear important [*a ~ thing*; *some ~ cause*]
dearn dread
dearth scarcity
death-practised whose death has been plotted
deathsman executioner
deboshed debauched
decay downturn
decline bend
deer animals
degree[1] extent [*such unnatural ~*]
degree[2] rank [*quality or ~*]
dejected cast down
delicate[1] sensitive [*the body's ~*]
delicate[2] cunning [*~ stratagem*]
demand request

demanded requested
demanding asking [*~ after you*]
denied forbade [*~ me to come in*]
deny refuse [*~ to speak*]
dependants attendants
depositaries trustees
deprive disinherit [*~ me*]
derogate degenerate
descry[1] sighting [*main ~*]
descry[2] make out [*~ the strength*]
desert worthy deed [*value her ~*]
deserving[1] reward [*fair ~; their ~s*]
deserving[2] worthiness [*study ~*]
desire ask [*~ him to go in*]
desired requested [*be then ~*]
desperate reckless [*~ train*]
desperately despairingly
detain keep back
determine make a decision
detested loathsome
difference[1] change [*~ and decay*]
difference[2] quarrel [*what is your ~*]
differences[1] distinctions of rank [*I'll teach you ~*]
differences[2] disagreements [*writ ... of ~*]
diffidences misgivings
diffuse disguise
digest take in
diligent persistent
dimensions organs
disbranch cut off
discerning distinguishing
disclaim disown
discommend find fault with
discover expose
discovery spying
disease disturbance of mind
dishonoured dishonourable
dislike disagreement
dismantle take away
disnatured unnatural

disordered disorderly
dispatch[1] hasty removal [*terrible ~*]
dispatch[2] dismissal [*attend ~*]
dispatch[3] deprive [*~ his nighted life*]
dispatch[4] deal with quickly [*~!*]
displayed behaved
disposition mood *or* state of mind
disquantity cut down
disquietly uneasily
dissipation dispersal
dissolution total destruction
dissolve melt into tears
distaff spindle
distaste dislike
distract mad
ditch-dog dead dog in a ditch
divinity theology
divisions disagreements [*~ in state*]
dog-hearted cruel
dolours sorrows
dominions territories
dotage senility
doubted feared [*to be ~*]
doubtful fearful
dower dowry
dowered endowed
dowerless lacking a dowry
dragon's tail orbit of the descending moon
dread terrifying [*~ exploit; ~ summit*]
dread-bolted with frightening thunderbolts
dreadful full of dread
drive hasten [*~ toward Dover*]
dull gloomy [*~ sight*]
duteous dutiful

ear hearing [*light of ~*]
ear-bussing ear-kissing
earnest pledge
effect, to in import
effects[1] signs [*large ~; ~ of courtesy*]

effects[2] results [*good ~; ~ he writes of; prove ~*]
elbows jostles
election choice
element place [*~'s below*]
elements forces of nature
elf tangle
embossed swollen
engine mechanical device
enguard protect
enjoy him sleep with him
enormous disorderly
enridged rippling
entertain employ
entertained treated
entertainment hospitality
entreat for intervene on behalf of
epicurism gluttony
equally impartially
equity justice
esperance hope
essay trial
estate situation
even o'er make sense of
event outcome
excellent supreme [*~ foppery*]
execution performance
exhibition allowance
expense spending
express show [*~ her goodliest*]
extremity utmost degree
eyeless blind

fain gladly *or* glad
faint feeble [*~ neglect*]
faintly very slightly
fair[1] beautiful *or* handsome
fair[2] just [*~ deserving*]
faith, in good faith in truth [mild swearword]
faithed believed
falchion curved broadsword

false[1] treacherous *or* faithless
false[2] wrong [*~ opinion; true or ~*]
false[3] wrongly [*~ persuaded*]
familiar unduly intimate [*be not ~*]
fancy[1] imagining [*each ~*]
fancy[2] love [*in my ~*]
fantastically fancifully
fares does
fare thee/ye/you well goodbye
fashion fit shape to my purposes
fast firm [*~ intent*]
fastened determined [*~ villain*]
father venerable sir [thou happy ~]
fathered was dealt with by a father
favours appearance [*hospitable ~*]
fearfully frighteningly
fear not don't worry
fears me frightens me
feel[1] react to [*~ wrongs*]
feel[2] test [*~ my affection*]
feeling heartfelt [*~ sorrows*]
feelingly in ways that reach the senses
feet footholds [*secret ~*]
felicitate made happy
fell[1] cruel [*~ motion*]
fell[2] skin [*flesh and ~*]
fellow companion [*who your ~ is*]
fen-sucked rising from marshes
festinate speedy
fetches stratagems
filths vile creatures
fine, in in conclusion
finical nit-picking
fire-new brand-new
fire us hence drive us away by fire
first, your your beginning
fit[1] fitting *or* suitable
fit[2] be *or* make suitable
fitchew polecat *or* prostitute
fitly[1] at the right time [*will ~ bring*]
fitly[2] fittingly [*may ~ like*]

fitness proper behaviour
flakes locks of hair
flashes moves abruptly
flawed broken
flaws fragments
fleshment first achievement
flesh ye initiate you
flourish [as stage direction] fanfare
flying-off desertion
foins sword-thrusts
fond foolish
fool[1] [play character] court jester
fool[2] darling [*my poor* ~]
footed[1] landed
footed[2] walked about
foppery foolishness
foppish foolish
fops fools
forbear[1] control myself [*I'll* ~]
forbear[2] stop [*dear sir,* ~]
forbear[3] avoid [~ *his presence*]
forbearance absence
fordid, fordone killed
fore-vouched previously declared
forfended forbidden
fork barbed arrow-head
forked having two legs
forks legs
forlorn wretched
form[1] formal procedure [~ *of justice*]
form[2] outward appearance [*for* ~]
forsooth certainly
foster nurse nurse who rears someone else's child
foulness immorality
frame[1] arrange [~ *the business*]
frame[2] condition [~ of nature]
framed created
frank generous [~ *heart*]
fraught filled
free untroubled [*mind's* ~; ~ *things*; ~ ... *thoughts*]

fret wear out
fretful angry
friendship friendly act
front forehead
frontlet frowning forehead
fruitfully plentifully
full[1] ideal [~ *issue*]
full[2] fully [*inform her* ~]
full[3] very [~ *sudddenly*; ~ *oft*]
fumiter type of weed
furnishings decorations
furrow-weeds weeds growing in ploughed furrows

gad, upon the suddenly
gait movement
gait, go your on your way
gale wind
gall[1] irritation [*pestilent* ~]
gall[2] bitterness [*added to the* ~]
gallow frighten
garb manner
gasted frightened
gate, go your on your way
generation family
generous mannerly
gentle[1] noble [~ *sir*]
gentle[2] kind [~ *wax*; ~ *and low*]
germens seeds
ghost spirit [*vex not his* ~]
gilded glittering
girdle waist
glance touch
glass mirror
glass eyes spectacles
glass-gazing admiring oneself in a mirror
goest travel on foot
goes to't copulates
goodliest best
goodman title for a man under the rank of gentleman

good years good times to come
gored deeply wounded
got begot
govern control
grace¹ favour [*without our* ~; *his* ~; *less* ~; *fickle* ~]
grace² honour [*with* ~; ~ *and person*; ~ *and a codpiece*; *to* ~ *him*]
grace³ success [~ *go with you*]
grace⁴ good quality [*in his own* ~]
grace, cry beg mercy
grace, your title for a Duke or King
graced stately
gracious¹ good [~ *aged man*]
gracious² used as a title of honour [~ *my lord*]
groom fellow
gross¹ vile [~ *crime*]
gross² large [~ *as beetles*]
grossly openly
grumble mumble
guessingly by guesswork
guilty of responsible for

habit clothing
halcyon kingfisher
half-blooded bastard
halter rope with a noose
handy-dandy make your choice
hap happen
haply perhaps
happy¹ fortunate [~ *father*; *most* ~; *write* ~]
happy² opportune [~ *hollow*]
hard¹ harsh [~ *rein*; ~ *house*; ~ *commands*; ~ *hearts*]
hard² close [~ *by here*]
hard³ difficult [*'tis* ~; ~ *cure*]
hard⁴ vigorously [*travelled* ~]
hard⁵ tightly [*bind...* ~]
hatch half-door
headier more headstrong

head-lugged pulled along by the ears
headpiece head-covering
heart courage [*valour and thy* ~]
heat, in the while feeling heated
heavy¹ weary [~ *eyes*]
heavy² sad [~ *case*]
heavy³ weighty [~ *substance*]
heavy⁴ serious [~ *causes*]
hell-hated hated as hell is hated
helm¹ covering of hair [*thin* ~]
helm² helmet [*plumed* ~]
hemlock type of poisonous plant
high important [~ *noises*]
high-engendered coming from the heavens
high-judging judging from on high
history story
hit agree *or* strive
hold¹ endure [*will you yet* ~]
hold² stop [~ *sir*]
holla¹ stop [as if to a horse]
holla² call out to [~ *the other*]
hollowness insincerity
home unsparingly [*charges* ~; *revenged* ~; *punish* ~]
honest chaste [~ *madam*]
honesty honour [*foolish* ~; *wears no* ~]
honoured honourable [~ *love*]
honours¹ noble rank [*mine* ~]
honours² honourable deeds [*your* ~]
honours, make them gain themselves renown
horn drinking-horn
horrible extremely [~ *steep*]
host lodging [*your good* ~]
hot¹ hot-tempered [~ *Duke*]
hot² enthusiastic [~ *questrists*; *not so* ~]
hotly ardently
hovel thee find yourself poor shelter
howe'er however great

hurricanoes water-spouts
hurtless without hurting
hysterica passio Latin for 'hysteria'

idle¹ mad [*~ old man*]
idle² unmoving [*~ pebble*]
idle³ useless [*~ and fond bondage; ~ weeds*]
ignobly shamefully
ignorance negligence
ill¹ bad [*~ thoughts*]
ill² badly [*~ affected; so ~; take it ~; well or ~; ill ~*]
ill³ unwell [*I am ~*]
image embodiment
imaginations delusions
immediacy being next in standing
imperfect¹ unfinished [*he left ~*]
imperfect² faulty [*senses grow ~*]
impertinency irrelevance
import signify [*~ my sister's letter*]
imports matters [*~ to the kingdom*]
importune urge
importuned pleading
impressed conscripted
improper unsuitable
in-a-door indoors
incense incite [*~ him*]
incline to support
indiscretion lack of judgement
indistinguished unimaginable
infirmities defects
inflamed fervent
ingenious alert
ingrateful ungrateful
inherit possess
injunction order
intelligence information
intelligent bearing information
intent intention
interested given a share
interest rights of possession

interlude short play staged to fill an interval
intermission interruption
intrince, intrinse intricate
invention scheme
issue¹ offspring [*~ of it; Albany's ~s; madam's ~; different ~s*]
issue² outcome [*full ~*]

jakes lavatory
jealous suspicious
joint-stool well-made stool
jovial majestic [like Jove]
judgement¹ opinion [*my ~*]
judgement² divine decision [*~ of the heavens*]
judgement³ good sense [*poor ~; thy dear ~*]
judgement⁴ judgement day [*to fear ~*]
judicious appropriate
Jug sweetheart [pet-name for Joan]
just¹ exact [*~ report*]
just² honourable [*repent to be ~; ~ proof*]
just³ legitimate [*~ and heavy causes*]
just⁴ righteous [*the heavens more ~; the gods are ~*]
justicer judge

kennel go outside to the dog-house
kibes chilblains
kind manner [*in that ~*]
kite bird of prey
knapped hit
knave¹ fellow [*this ~; pretty ~; fool and ~*]
knave² servant [*my ~; friendly ~; his ~*]
knave³ rogue [*~s; lord's ~; more ~; a ~; beastly ~; plain ~; ancient ~*]
knee, to to kneel before

labours services

lag of lagging behind
lances horse soldiers armed with a lance
large[1] impressive sounding [~ *speeches*]
large[2] generous [~*st bounty*; ~ *effects*]
latched nicked
late recent *or* recently
late, of recently
lecher copulate [*does ~*]
lendings borrowings
let-alone power to interfere
lethargied subdued
levied enlisted
light of ear ready to listen [to wicked things]
light on fall on
lights on comes across
like[1] likely [~ *to have*; ~ *to hear*; ~ *to be*]
like[2] equal [*take ~ hold*]
like[3] please [*fitly ~*; *~s me not*]
like, the the same
likeness appearance
Lipsbury pinfold held between my teeth
list[1] listen to [~ *a brief tale*]
list[2] wish [~ *to grace him*]
lists musters
litter portable bed
little-seeming worthless *or* disrespectful
living livelihood
loathly with such loathing
long-ingraffed long-implanted
look about be on the look-out
looked not for didn't expect
look him find him
looped full of holes
lose thee nothing not harm you at all
louse become lice-infested
low humble [~ *farms*; ~ *correction*]

lowness decline
lubber clumsy dolt
lurk keep hidden
lust-dieted pleasure-gorged
lusty vigorous
luxury lechery
lym male [hound]

machination plotting
madded maddened
made good secured
made intent resolved plan
main mainland
mainly entirely
make from avoid *or* release
make nothing of treat as worthless
makes not up isn't settled
maledictions cursing
man, more more manliness
mantle covering
mar ruin
mark notice *or* pay attention to
marvel wonder
mate and make husband and wife
material full of substance
mates companions
matter[1] substance *or* subject-matter
matter[2] meaning [*wield the ~*]
mature ready
maugre in spite of
meads meadows
mean mean to do [*what do you ~*]
meanest of lowest rank
meaning intention
meat edible part
meats scraps
meet right and proper [*judge it ~*; *me's ~*; *think ~*]
meiny household retinue
memories reminders
mend amend
mere[1] personal [~ *defects*]

mere[2] complete [~ *fetches*]
messes dishes
methinks, methought it seems / seemed to me
mettle spirit
milk-livered cowardly
minces gives an affected impression of
minikin shrill *or* dainty
ministers messengers
miscarry come to harm
mischief harm
misconstruction misunderstanding
miscreant heretic
modest moderate
moiety share
monopoly sole trading right
monsters it makes a monster of it
moonshines months
mopping and mowing grimacing and making faces
moral full of moral sentiments
morrow morning
mortified dead to feeling
motion [in fencing] attack
motley distinctive dress of a fool
mowing making faces
musters mobilizing of troops
mutinies riots

natural feeling proper affection
natural fool simpleton by nature
naughty[1] wicked [~ *lady*]
naughty[2] nasty [~ *night*]
nearly especially
neat posh
neighboured acquainted
nether earthly
nether-stocks stockings for the lower leg
nicely scrupulously
nighted blacked-out

nimble sudden
nine-fold set of nine attendants
noises reports
noiseless peaceful
note regard
nothing nobody [~ *almost*]
nothing, in in no particular
notice recognition [*place or* ~]
notion understanding
nuncle master [= 'mine uncle']

O, an a nothing
object sight
obscured disguised
observants ingratiating attendant
occasion[1] reason [~ ... *of some poise*; *further* ~]
occasion[2] circumstances [*breed from hence* ~]
occupation calling
oeillades amorous glances
o'erlook read through
o'er-looking perusal
o'er-read read through
o'erskip jump lightly over
o'ertake catch up to
o'erwatched exhausted from lack of sleep
offend us harm us
office task
office, in if given status
oft often
ope open
open displayed [banner]
operation influence
operative effective
opposeless unable to be resisted
opposite[1] opposed [*loathly* ~]
opposite[2] opponent [*the* ~*s*; *unknown* ~]
orbs stars
order normal procedure

ordinance decree
out, been been away from home
outface defy
outjest overcome with the force of jokes
out-paramoured had more lovers than
outscorn overcome by mockery
outstorm rage more violently than a storm
out-wall external appearance
outward worth wealth
over *see also* **o'er**
overlusty too vigorous
overture disclosure
owes possesses

pack depart
packings plottings
packs gangs
pain effort [*your* ~]
pander pimp
parricides murders of fathers
partial biased
particular private [~ *fear*, ~ *broils*]
particular, his himself
parti-eyed with eyes of mixed colours
parts qualities [*rarest* ~]
pass¹ juncture [*to this* ~]
pass² pass sentence [~ *upon his life*]
pass³ pass away [*might he* ~]
paste pastry
pat opportunely
patience composure [~ *and sorrow*]
patient calm [~ *thoughts*]
patiently with fortitude
patrimony estate
pattern model
pawn, pawn down pledge
peace be still [*would not* ~]
peascod pea-pod
pelican bird reputed to feed her young with her own blood

pell-mell in headlong confusion
pelting paltry
pendulous overhanging
penning handwriting
perchance perhaps
perdu sentinel exposed to danger
perfect mature [~ *age*]
perforce¹ forcibly [*again* ~]
perforce² of necessity [*from me* ~; *itself* ~; *must* ~; ~ *must*]
peril, at at risk of punishment
period¹ fitting conclusion [*seemed a* ~]
period² aim [*point and* ~]
philosopher sage
physic medicine
picture description
pieced added
piece out increase
pight determined
pilgrimage journey
pillicock penis
pinfold place for keeping stray animals
place¹ position [*our* ~; *thy* ~; *my* ~; *strength* ~]
place² lodging [~ *or notice*]
plackets skirt openings
plain complain [*cause to* ~]
plainness plain-speaking
plate armour
pleasant pleasurable [~ *vices*]
pleasures intentions [*greater* ~]
plight pledge
plighted hidden *or* solemnly pledged
pluck upon bring to ruin
point purpose [~ *and period*]
point, at in readiness
poise weight
politic prudent
politician schemer
ponderous weighty

porridge meat and vegetable stew

port gateway

portable bearable

portion dowry

post¹ courier [*reeking* ~; *our* ~*s*; ~ *unsanctified*]

post² hasten [~ *speedily*; ~*ed*]

potency authority

potential powerful

power god [*the* ~ *that made me*]

powers armed forces

practice¹ scheme [*my* ~*s*; *damned* ~; *is* ~ *only*]

practice² trickery [*his* ~; *this is* ~]

practised on plotted against

pranks outrageous behaviour

precedent example

precipitating plunging

predominance ascendancy

preferment promotion

pregnant¹ well-disposed [~ *to good pity*]

pregnant² meaningful [*very* ~]

preparation force ready for war

prepared drawn

presages indicates

prescribed limited

presented displayed

presently at once

press-money money paid to conscripted recruits

pretence plan

pretty fine [~ *fellow*]

prevent forestall [~ *the fiend*]

prey preying [*lion in* ~]

price me value myself

pricks spikes

pride splendour [*borrowed* ~]

privily privately

proclaimed officially declared to be an outlaw

profess¹ as an occupation [*thou* ~]

profess² declare [*I* ~]

professed with avowed affection

profession solemn vow

proof¹ making good [*just* ~]

proof² evidence [~ *and precedent*]

proof, in to the test

proper¹ typical [~ *deformity*]

proper² good-looking [*so* ~]

propinquity close kinship

prosper it make it prosperous

prove make trial *or* test [*I'll* ~; *to* ~]

provided prepared

provision supply of necessities

publish announce

published proclaimed

pudder hubbub

puissant powerful

purpose plan

purpose, to the to the point at issue

purposed intended *or* intending

purpose not intend not to do what I say

qualified moderated [~ *the heat*]

qualities accomplishments

quality¹ nature [*fierce* ~; ~ *of nothing*; *fiery* ~; *depraved a* ~]

quality² rank [*your* ~; *man of* ~]

queasy uncertain *or* delicate

question¹ point at issue [*queasy* ~]

question² discussion [*bear* ~]

question³ dispute [*come to* ~]

question⁴ conversation [*verbal* ~]

questrists seekers

quicken revive

quit¹ avenge [~ *this horrid act*]

quit² bear yourself [~ *you well*]

rack limb-stretching torture machine

rage madness [*ungoverned* ~; *great* ~]

rail rant

raiment clothing

rake up bury
rank[1] gross [~ ... *riots*]
rank[2] stinking [~ *fumiter*]
rare unusual
rash force *or* slash with [~ *boarish fangs*]
ratsbane rat poison
ravish tear from
razed altered
reasoned brought up
recreant heretic
redress remedy
reeking sweaty
regards considerations
rein control
relieve aid
remainders remaining people
remediate healing
rememberest remind
remotion departure
remove change of residence
renege deny
repeals recalls
reposal placing
reprovable blameworthy
required requested
reservation keeping back
reserve retain
resolution certainty
resolve inform
respect, upon with consideration
retention confinement
revenue income
reverb reverberate
reverence[1] respect [~ *of age; no* ~]
reverence[2] respected state [*whose* ~; ~ *made*]
reverend revered
rigour strength
rings eye-sockets
ripe red and full [~ *lip*]
rivalled competed

rive open up
roguish wild
roundest bluntest
rubbed hindered
rude stormy
ruffle[1] handle roughly [~ *thus*]
ruffle[2] rage [*sorely* ~]

sad downcast
safe redress certain remedy
safer sense sound mind
sallets salads
salt salt tears
samphire type of marine plant
sapient wise
satisfaction removal of doubt
savour[1] nature [*much o'the* ~]
savour[2] relish [*filths* ~]
saw wise saying [*common* ~]
say [= assay] evidence
scant[1] curtail [~ *my sizes*]
scant[2] neglect [~ *her duty*]
scanted neglected
scape escape
scattered disunited
scurvy contemptible
season, out of inconveniently
seasons times of year
seconds supporters
sectary devotee
sects factions
secure us make us over-confident
seeming outward behaviour
see that look into that
seize on/upon take possession of
self same
self-covered self-concealing
self-subdued unresisting
semblance appearance
sense[1] feeling [*square of* ~; *vile* ~]
sense[2] power of reason [*safer* ~; *bereaved* ~]

sentence pronouncement
sepulchring serving as a burial-place for
sequent following
serviceable diligent
servile slavish
servingman male servant
sesey [in hunting] off you go
set less don't stake too much
set my rest rely for my repose
several various
shadowy shady
shanks legs
sheepcotes buildings where sheep shelter
shelled without a shell
shift change
shivered smashed to pieces
shoot let fly
shortens makes ineffective
shows displays [*happy* ~]
shrill-gorged shrill-sounding
side-piercing heart-rending
silly-ducking foolishly bowing
simple common
simple answered direct in reply
simples medicines
simular pretender
sinews nerves
single unaided
sith that since
sizes allowances
skill discernment
slack¹ less attentive [*come* ~]
slack² neglect [*to* ~ *ye*]
slaves enslaves
slenderly poorly
slipshod wearing slippers
sliver split off
smilets slight smiles
smile you do you laugh at
smilingly with a smile

smokes gives off steam [blood]
smooth humour
smug neat
snuff smouldering candle-end
snuffs huffs
soiled lively
sojourn stay
something somewhat [~ *saucily*; ~ *fears*]
sometime¹ former [~ *daughter*]
sometime² sometimes [~ *with*; ~ *in*]
soothe humour
sop piece of soggy bread
sophisticated removed from the simple state
sore severe
sorely severely
sot blockhead
sovereign overpowering
space¹ possession of property [*dearer than ... ~*; *no less in* ~]
space² expanse [~ *of woman's will*]
space³ space of time [*further* ~]
speak reprove [*I may* ~]
speak for cry out for
speculations observers
speed prosper [*letter* ~; ~ *you*]
spherical of the spheres [stars]
spill destroy
spite of intermission despite being interrupted
spleen bad temper
spoil ravage
sport recreation
spurn reject
square normal condition
squiny squint
squire attendant on a nobleman
squire-like like an attendant
stake¹ place of execution [*coward to the* ~]
stake² post [*tied to the* ~]

standing stagnant
stand's act as his
stand the course withstand attacks by dogs
stand up confront boldly
star-blasting bad influence of the stars
stars fortunes [*great* ~]
started hurried
starts outbursts
stealth[1] stealing [*fox in* ~]
stealth[2] stealing away [~ *of nature*]
stelled starry
steward controller of domestic affairs
stewed drenched
stiff unresponsive
still ever *or* always
still-soliciting always begging
stir move about
stirs moves
stocked put in the stocks
stocking putting in the stocks
stock-punished punished by being put in the stocks
stone mineral used as a mirror
stople stop up
store abundance
straight at once
strain quality
strained excessive
strangered with made a stranger to
strength resources [*in my* ~]
stretch strain to the utmost [~ *their duties*]
strokes afflictions
sub-contracted already betrothed
subdued brought down
subscribe concur
subscription obedience *or* approval
succeed follow on
success result
sue beg

suffer[1] bear [*cannot* ~]
suffer[2] allow [~ *you*]
sufferance distress
suffered tolerated [*as it is* ~]
suffers undergoes [*it* ~]
suggestion temptation
suit entreaty
suited dressed
summoners court-officers who ensure attendance
sumpter pack-horse
superfluous over-supplied
superflux superfluity
super-serviceable officious
supposed pretended
surfeits excesses
surgeons doctors
surrender giving up of power
sway[1] controlling influence, guiding power [*sweet* ~; *i'the* ~]
sway[2] position of authority [*the* ~]
sways controls [~ *not*]
sword soldier [*become a* ~]

taint discredit
taking[1] infectious [~ *airs*]
taking[2] attack of disease [*and* ~]
taking[3] being arrested [*my* ~]
taking-off killing
tall fine
tardiness hesitancy
tarry stay
tax censure
teem give birth
tell count out [~ *in a year*; ~ *their gold*]
temper[1] stable mind [*in* ~]
temper[2] soften [~ *clay*]
temperance self-control
tend attend
tended upon waited upon
tender[1] care [*the* ~]

tender² offer [~ *less*]
tender-hefted tender-hearted
tends awaits
text theme
thought-executing acting as fast as thought *or* thought-destroying
threading tracing a path through
threat threaten
three-suited allowed three suits a year
thrilled pierced
thrusting on imposition
thwart perverse
tike cur
time lifetime [*soundest of his ~; best of our ~s*]
time, in good at the right moment
tithing parish
title claim
toad-spotted spotted like a toad [as if with poison]
todpole tadpole
token sign
Tom o'Bedlam madman
touch¹ affect [~ *me with*]
touch² taint [*cannot ~ me*]
touch, in my by my touching you
touches affects [~ *us*]
toward in preparation
train retinue
tranced in a trance
transport carry off
treachers traitors
trice brief period
trick distinctiveness
trilled rolled
troop with go along with
troth plight make a solemn promise
trowest accept as true
trundle-tail dog with a trailing tail
trunk body
tune state of mind

Turlygod nonsense name used by Edgar
turn, brain head becomes dizzy
tyrannous cruel
tyranny cruelty [~ *of the open night*]

unable inadequate
unaccommodated unclothed
unbolted unsifted
unbonneted bare-headed
unconstant changeable
understanding knowledge
undertake take responsibility
undo do away with [~ *excess*]
unfee'd unpaid
unfold reveal
unfriended friendless
ungoverned uncontrolled
ungracious wicked
unhappily wretchedly
unkind lacking in family affection
unkindness ingratitude
unnumbered countless
unpossessing unable to inherit property
unprized-precious priceless
unprovided unprotected
unpublished concealed
unquietly restlessly
unremovable immovable
unsanctified unholy
unstate give up everything
unsubstantial intangible
untender unkind
untented too deep to be cleansed with lint
untimely at a bad time
untuned out-of-tune
upward top part [~ *of thy head*]
use¹ profit [*no ~ of nothing*]
use² outcome [*deadly ~*]
use³ treat [~ *thee*; ~ *me*; ~ *them*]

usurer money-lender
usurp take wrongful possession of

vain stupid [~ *fool*]
validity value
vantage right moment
varlet rogue
vary variation
vassal slave
vault roof
vaunt-curriers announcers
venge avenge
vent utter
venture run a risk
vex afflict
vexed stormy
vicious depraved
vile[1] shameful [~ *sense*]
vile[2] worthless [~ *things*]
villain-like like a servant *or* rogue
villein servant
virtue[1] chastity [*simular of* ~]
virtue[2] powers [*unpublished* ~]
virtue[3] courage [*single* ~]
visage face
vor dialect form of 'warn'
vulgar generally known

wage[1] risk [*pawn to* ~]
wage[2] struggle [*choose to* ~]
wagtail bower and scraper
wake wakefulness [*asleep and* ~; *sleep to* ~]
wakes fetes [~ *and fairs*]
wall-newt lizard on the wall
want need
want not does not fall short
wanton badly behaved [~ *boys*]
wantons wilful creatures
ward someone under protection
warped distorted
warrant assurance

watch stay awake [*to* ~; *have* ~*d*]
watches is on the look-out [*my father* ~]
water water-newt [*and the* ~]
waterish full of water *or* wishy-washy
wawl howl
waywardness perversity
weal state
wear out survive [*we'll* ~]
web and the pin disease of the eye
weeds clothes
weight affliction
welked twisted
well-compact well-formed
well favoured good-looking
wenches girls
whistling calling
white[1] fresh [~ *herring*]
white[2] ready for harvesting [~ *wheat*]
wholesome[1] health-giving [~ *weal*]
wholesome[2] reasonable [~ *end*]
whoremaster lecherous
whoreson bastard
wide confused
wide-skirted with wide borders
wield express
wind me into him pursue a devious course for me
wind up put in order
windowed full of holes
wisdom judgement
wisdom, man's human knowledge
wit mental ability
wit, by by cunning
wits, five wits faculties of mind or body
wold rolling hills
wolvish wolfish
wont accustomed
worser more evil
worships honours
worsted made of woollen fabric

worth means [*outward* ~]
worthied him gave honour to him
writ written [*hath / have* ~]
writ, my warrant
wrongs insults
wrought brought about

yeoman land-holding farmer
yoke-fellow fellow-worker

zir dialect form of 'sir'
zo dialect form of 'so'
zwaggered dialect form of 'swaggered'
[= bullied]